MY UNSPOKEN THOUGHTS
AND EMOTIONS

MY UNSPOKEN THOUGHTS AND EMOTIONS

ELIZABETH REHEMMA

Charleston, SC
www.PalmettoPublishing.com

My Unspoken Thoughts and Emotions

First Edition

Paperback ISBN: 979-8-8229-0693-8
eBook ISBN: 979-8-8229-0694-5

CONTENTS

TWO TEARS

One lonely tear rolls down my cheek.

I wonder where you are.

I can hardly bear to speak.

You said you'd never be far.

Nothing's the same since you've been gone, even the rain is a
downpour of pain.

I sigh;

I cry

You didn't even say goodbye.

I'm like a fading flower in need of a gentle spring shower.

What I need to know is when you will be back.

Without you, happiness I lack.

Just to see your smile, I would run a thousand miles.

So beautiful, so bright, the most wonderful sight.

Now a smile has spread across my face, and for sadness there
is no more space.

One lonely tear rolls down my cheek; now, because of bliss,
as I realize never did I need to miss you.

You never did part, for you have always been and will
eternally live in my heart.

STORMS

I thought I had known sadness;
I thought I had known pain.
At the time, it was just the opposite of gladness,
A thing that seldom came.
I knew not of misery, desperation, and anxiety.
Little did I know of what the future had in store for me.
It wasn't abrupt;
It did not hit all at once.
It started tapping lightly on the ground, like ants marching
      all around.
Slowly but surely it increased, and hardly did it ever cease.
That light drizzle turned to a storm and had me oh so very torn.
That downpour of pain drove me nearly insane.
It seemed as though I was often distraught.
Happiness and peace were things I had lost.
I walked alone for so long, wondering if I could carry on.
Perpetual lethargy and constant misery were those with
      which I had camaraderie.
The place I once associated with joy became a sick twisted
      game in which I was the toy.
Every day was a monotonous blur.

At one point I had stopped feeling,

Yet at the same time, I was growing more and more insecure,
and the empty ache had me reeling.

Everyone thought my silence was simply because I was shy.

Truth be told, that wasn't it; I was dead behind the eyes.

I forced a smile, faked a laugh, and no one failed to fall for
my act.

"I'm fine, really. No, I'm just tired" was my everyday anthem.

They all bought it or simply didn't care enough to notice that
the true me was slipping away, and left in her place
was a phantom.

I was beyond depressed.

I was lifeless and numb.

But a child through all this, such a wreck and too young.

Looks can be deceiving.

I know this just from knowing me.

A happy person who had it all together; I was the epitome.

It was such a horrid nightmare, if only it had been a bad
dream.

I was entirely consumed with despair, wishing I would wake
at any moment with simply a scare.

Unfortunately it was all too real, too endless, like a hideous
maze leading a million different ways.

Oh the sorrow, the agony, it had truly shattered me.

How could they not care?

How could they be so ruthless?

It was far from fair, and left me utterly hopeless.

No longer was I simply sinking into that bottomless pit of pain.

I had reached a point where I was free-falling, and I didn't
fight it.

There was nothing to gain.

The place I once loved and cherished so dearly became the
bane of my life and left me so weary.

I hoped in vain for change, but everything stayed quite the same.

My anguish wasn't even tamed.

I was far from okay; this was each and every day.

I hadn't done anything to deserve it; why did I have to pay?

It didn't have to be that way.

That time was tumultuous.

It's a wonder how I functioned.

Every minute was strenuous.

I felt I was under destruction.

I wouldn't have wished my life upon anyone, especially not
on someone just as young.

It couldn't even have been called a life.

It was more of a miserable existence.

I was breathing but not living, and sadly wishing for death's
arrival.

No longer did I care for survival.

Yes, I had lost the will to live; I had no more fight to give.

Nevertheless, I pushed on.

I knew there was something greater just beyond.

QUESTIONS

I have a question.
What did I ever do?
Draw attention?
You know very well that's not true.
I was silent, let alone quiet.
I always kept to myself.
Your glares that were so violent are what made me move in
      stealth.
I went out of my way to keep out of yours, rerouting my
      path, hiding behind doors.
I was always so nice and polite, and always opted for flight
      rather than fight.
I tried to look okay, and I always stayed at bay.
What was the reason for this torment when your little gain
      was so transient?
I never asked for you to like me, or even to be nice.
I just wanted you to leave me alone as I stood there frozen
      like ice.
Each time you passed, I held my breath, hoping for the best
      as I turned to look away, until it was safe and until it
      was okay.

Did you ever consider what your words and actions may do,
    or even the pain you put me through?
Did you ever ponder how I might feel, or how long the
    damage you'd done would take to heal?
Sticks and stones may break and bruise my bones, but all
    that goes away.
Your malicious words and cruel glowers certainly don't do the
    same.
How don't you understand or care that you left me
    crumbling like sand and in despair?
I was broken,
I was in pieces, because of those horrid words you had spoken.
The agony was seldom ceasing.
You pointed out my flaws as if I did not already see them.
You had me fighting back tears again and again.
I was drowning in my tears and imprisoned by my fears.
I felt desperate and forlorn.
My heart was oh so very torn.
It's said that everything happens for a reason and that what
    doesn't kill you makes you stronger.
Yes, I'm a better person, but was the extent of this misery
    necessary in the long run, when it left me wishing I
    was dead?
I guess I'll just have to trust that somehow it was, as I
    continue to search for the rainbow's end.

UNTIL YOU KNOW

You never know who has your back until hard times fall, and when you look around, there's no one to call. The very ones who claimed they would always stay the same suddenly switch up and won't pay you the time of day. You never know who has your back until you find yourself in lack: lack of happiness, of peace, and whatever feeds their selfish greed, until you're the one in need of precisely what you gave, naively believing that they would do the same. To your surprise, they don't; they simply disappear, leaving you wondering and unclear if what you shared was even real, or if instead it was all in your head, a mere figment of your imagination that existed for a duration of time, but only in your mind, not in reality. In actuality you were the only one you could count on through the ups and downs. You never know who really cares until you end up in despair and in search of a shoulder to cry on, until you learn to dry your own tears and be strong. You never know who's even true until life's troubles start to brew, unwavering sadness then ensues; one trial after the other leaves you battered and bruised and without a clue as to whether you'll win the fight or lose. You never know about your might until, in the pursuit of a glimmer of light, you finally find both inside. It's sad to discover that no one has you like you do, but this so-bering truth may help you get through, unburdened with the weight of having to keep a brave face, put up a facade, fool people with a mirage, and constantly have to pretend to be okay, day after day. In all honesty, it can be a bit lonely, but amidst it you find authenticity. The ones who remain by your side will be with you through rain or shine. Even if you find yourself alone, don't take it as a loss. You gained clarity on those around you, and whether they would stick with you or not. You never know who has your back until life's trials and put all to test; unlock your inner strength, and introduce you to your truest friend: yourself.

NO NEED FOR CHEAP TALK

What gives you the right to make lewd remarks when I or
     any other woman walks by?
You could have stayed silent; you could have kept to yourself
     or left it at a simple "Hi."
When we walk down the street, you see us as meat and get
     the funny idea that we're your little treat.
You whistle and call, expecting an answer. You honk and
     shout, as though that's ever worked out.
Have you ever considered the discomfort and fear that
     you cause, or maybe that your comments are not
     compliments at all?
Do you really think your vulgar words are what we want to
     hear, or that we actually like it when you leer?
Did it ever occur to you that we don't want to know what
     you'd like to do?
Or that when we ignore you, it's not that we didn't hear you
     but hoped that you'd get a clue?
News flash: when we got ready that day, it wasn't for you, so
     kindly stay away.
Okay? You got it?

And by the way, I'm not interested, so you might as well stay
in your lane.
Just so you know, your crude words aren't getting you far, so
keep walking, keep moving, and keep driving that car.
And heads up, just because our clothes might be tight,
doesn't mean we gave you an invite.
Would you make such remarks and sounds with your mom
around? If not, then how 'bout you don't do so now.
Also, just because our outfit is fitting, doesn't mean that we're
yours for the picking.
We're not out in the wild, so stop stalking us like prey; it hasn't
worked out before, and it's not going to work out today.
I'm not "baby."
I'm not "sexy."
I'm a stranger to you, so keep walking; we both have better
things to do.
I'm not sure what you were hoping to accomplish.
Did you want attention? Well hey, you got it.
Would you like a standing ovation, because that's all you're
getting—and nothing more, that's for sure.
So the next time you feel the need to yell out sexual
obscenities, stop and ponder the words that you
speak, and question whether they uplift or demean.

WHEN TIME STOOD STILL

The first time I saw him, my heart fluttered and raced.

The first time our eyes met, my breath caught in its place.

The first time he spoke to me, my head spun dizzily.

The first time he touched me, my nerves went into a frenzy.

Yes, I remember it as though it were yesterday.

Never before had I ever felt that way.

The tension was palpable, the intensity overwhelming.

My instant fall for him was irrevocable; I thought I must
have been dreaming.

He was kind and he was caring; he was funny and sweet.

He was tall and he was charming, and for the eyes quite a
treat.

I'm not sure what captivated me more: his steady stare, or his
smile, which I adore.

I didn't want to take my eyes off of him, but I couldn't help
looking at the floor.

His dreamy eyes, his beautiful face, the way he looked at me.

It all took me to cloud nine immediately and made me feel as
I never had before.

It was love at first sight; I cannot deny it. In that moment I
reached new heights.

Each time I looked at him, he was already staring; I was so
      beyond happy, my heart was nearly tearing.
The way he looked at me left me in ecstasy.
The way he made me feel was somewhat unreal.
He had cast a spell on me and stolen my heart.
It happened instantly, and that was only the start.

12:45

I had read about the phenomenon of love at first sight in romance novels. I had watched it play out in movie scenes and heard people recount their encounters of it in their own stories. I always believed in it and dreamed of experiencing it. When it arrived, I was taken by surprise that it was just as it was described in love songs, that it is just as dreamlike as it seemed in movies, and that it was as remarkable as it was said to be in novels. I was taken by your beauty: there was just so much to take in, from the planes of your beautiful face to your tall, strong frame. That moment was truly amazing and like nothing I had ever experienced. As soon as we were informally introduced and I turned to look at you, I was locked in your gaze as you were in mine, and our surroundings seemed to dissipate. It was just you and I, frozen in place, staring into each other's eyes as space and time briefly ceased to exist. I thought that when people said time stands still when you meet your soulmate, they only meant it figuratively. But I think they were speaking literally, because in that instant, when we first set eyes on each other, time froze as we momentarily stepped into an alternate realm, where we were enveloped in wonder and oblivious to all else except for each other's presence. That moment couldn't have lasted more than a few short seconds, yet so much happened in that minuscule amount of time. It's like in your eyes I recognized someone I had never met before. I was certain that this was our first encounter, because I would have definitely remembered you. Yet there was a curious sense of familiarity between us. What amplified this experience was that everything I felt was mirrored by your facial expression. There in front of me was a beautiful reflection of every emotion that was coursing through me. It's as though in that moment there was a poetic juxtaposition of a question and a realization, just as my mind asked, "Who is he?" my heart said, "There he is..." and something that's hard to describe was ignited. It wasn't just excitement, it was more than interest, and it wasn't simply physical attraction—though that definitely weighed in. It was like...as we stood staring into each other's eyes, our souls reached forward toward one another, longing to embrace after a lengthy separation, and something that had previously lain dormant was awakened. That something was a combination of soul-deep, electrifying love like I had never felt before, intense magnetic attraction that I hadn't known existed, and something else that I can't quite find the words for. Perhaps it was the sense that something bigger than us had just happened. Reflecting back on it, that was exactly the case: something greater than us had taken place that day. The first time I looked into your beautiful, piercing eyes, it was like the stars aligned and the earth beneath my feet shifted. My lips parted a bit, as did yours, and for a moment it seemed as though I would float up off the floor. The feeling was surreal and entirely dreamlike; it even seemed like a warm, velvety blanket of love wrapped us up and everything outside it was nonexistent. The only concrete thing in that moment was you and I, frozen in time in a state of enchantment as we gazed into each other's eyes. When that brief but impactful moment passed and we were finally back from that fantastical place, time seemed to elapse much faster to make up for having stood still, and the silence surrounding us broke. I inhaled deeply after having had my breath catch in its place, upon seeing your beautiful face. I hardly knew what to make of what had just taken place; all I knew was that I had to know you. The moments thereafter only heightened this desire. That day was laden with many firsts: another was when you were staring at me from across the room, and though we weren't making eye contact, since I was talking to a friend, it felt like your gaze would set me ablaze; I felt so faint. When you walked over and spoke to me, I couldn't breathe: I couldn't believe that you were even more beautiful up close. I could hardly hear my own words over the ringing in my ears; everything around you sort of blurred. I thought I would burst. You took my breath away and had me absolutely enamored. Words can't properly capture the state of rapture I was in; the expression on your handsome face as you gazed at me filled me with sheer bliss. Never before had someone's stare alone electrified my entire being. Each time you focused your eyes on me, either from up close or at a minor distance, it felt like electrical impulses were shooting through me producing bursts of ecstasy. I could hardly fathom that eye contact was the reason for all this, or that such a minor amount of time had just had such an effect on me like nothing else I had experienced in all my life. I wouldn't have been surprised to suddenly rise and find that it had merely been a dream, but thankfully it was real, because I wouldn't want to imagine having had such a surreally beautiful experience only for it to vanish just as suddenly as it happened. What's better still is that to my surprise and great delight, the excitement and intensity didn't subside after we initially locked eyes. It continued to rise as the day progressed, as did the intrigue regarding what had just happened. I still can't precisely describe what exactly happened, but what I do know is that in that instant, two souls who were destined to be finally met in a moment long awaited. It's funny how even though my nerves were in a frenzy and I could hardly think or breathe when you first spoke to me, it was still so sublime, and to this day those moments remain unrivaled. I've relived those moments in my mind countless times; they were so splendid I didn't want any of it to end. However, there's one ending I wasn't melancholy about, and that was at last reaching the end of my journey to find love. I hadn't been actively seeking, but I was so anxiously awaiting, and there at last when I laid eyes on you, my heart and soul knew that the one I had always dreamed of meeting had finally been found, on that fateful Monday, October the Twentieth of Twenty-Fourteen, at approximately Twelve Forty-Five.

UNQUESTIONABLY DESTINED

Love of my life, do the occurrences surrounding our relationship intrigue you as much as they do me? Because there are
innumerable curious events that leave me feeling there's more
to this than it seems—the first one being the moment we met.
I don't believe in past lives, but I must confide: that moment
alone makes me wonder at times. Despite being strangers there
was a peculiar sense of familiarity between us coupled with the
excitement present upon first locking eyes. When we're together there's always a sign we're right where we ought to be;
it's plain to see. Nothing is forced, everything flows with ease,
and on top of that, there's so much chemistry. While it's un-
likely to find us in the same circles, it's as though we've always
known each other. It's as if we've always been friends, but more
than friends since before we met. It's like that day we first
locked eyes wasn't the first time but rather the first time after
a long while. It was like we could finally continue where we
left off and grow what we had cultivated long ago and live the
life we had dreamed of once upon a time. Does it puzzle you
that people speak of falling in love gradually after their first
encounter with the person they describe as the one, while with
you and me it was instantaneous? Do you ever wonder about

how we always find ourselves together, like something larger is at play and we're being led to be with each other? Because I do. I can't shake the deep inner conviction that we're destined to be together forever, building upon what we started a lifetime or lifetimes ago, now long forgotten, but that we're somewhat and somehow reminded of each time we look into each other's eyes. True love of mine, when we're together, there's always a sign we're right where we ought to be, it's plain to see. Nothing is forced, everything flows with ease: the way it should be for all eternity.

LOVESTRUCK

I didn't know it was possible to love someone this much until I met you. My love for you grows and grows exponentially, leaving me worried that one day my heart may just burst from the magnitude of my love for you. I truly love you to the point that it sometimes creates an ache in my chest. It takes my breath away when I'm reminded of the passionate love between us. It's so deep; it's so strong. There's no question that it's lifelong and beyond, somehow, I'll continue to love you. It just wasn't feasible that I would end up loving someone unconditionally, in every sense of the word, but time has proven there are no limits at which I will stop loving you more and more, regardless of all else. You set my heart ablaze with your gaze and keep this fire in me burning for you night and day; it remains and shows no sign of fading away. It's so great; it's so strong. There's no question that it's lifelong and beyond, somehow, I'll continue to love you. A sweet melody springs from my heart, and our love is what's inspired it. My darling, let's never part. We can scour the earth and never find a love like ours. Come what may, be it good or bad, I'm in it for the long run, for better for worse. This isn't short term; you know I'm yours, just yours, because this love I have for you is so deep, so strong. There's no question that it's lifelong and beyond, somehow, I'll continue to love you. Love of my life, for you to get a deeper sense of my love and devotion, let me describe my love for you in greater detail so you can taste how I feel. I love you with every bit of me; when I see you, I melt instantly. When I hear my name on your lips, it thrills me. My nerves go into a frenzy whenever you're in close proximity. My heart beats wildly when you merely stand close to me. Thoughts of you play in my brain on a loop, and with every fiber of my being, I love you even more than living. I didn't know it was possible to love someone this much until I met you.

WHO DO YOU THINK YOU ARE?

Who do you think you are to try and have your cake and eat it too? You're now with someone else yet try to talk to me like nothing's new. I can't believe the disrespect; you flirt with me, then you're on to the next. It's as though you're on a quest to put my patience to the test. If that's the case, then be my guest, but don't be shocked when it's gotten less, and you come to find that, after all, I've lost interest. I can't believe this disregard. You take my heart then just discard it, pick it up again only to scar it. Honestly, what's with you? You act like you're so nice, but we both know that's not true: with me you're as cold as ice. I just don't understand. To me, this is out of hand. Or do you think it's your right and that I should just sit tight, sit down, wait around? If that's the case, then I'm astounded. Your audacity confounds me. Do you honestly believe this is how you ought to treat me? If that's the case, then—my mistake. I guess I was wrong. I should have never placed my hope where it did not belong. It's too bad, though, because I really thought that we would be together, especially when I consider the first time we met each other. Reluctantly—no, certainly—I feel it's time to put "us" to rest, for what once was is now most certainly dead. I am more than fed up, so get up and leave me alone. Your mistreatment is simply something I can no longer condone. Time and time again, you've shown me that I'm only an option. So it's time you learned the lesson that you should have acted with caution, as opposed to the endless indecision and inconsistency that inevitably lead me to dread being around you, strikingly contrary to the time I longed to be wherever you were. Unfortunately, you chose her, and her, and her, and her. To say the least, that was regrettable; I'm sure you can concur. But these are the choices you've made, and in your bed you must lie. Don't think that when you return— oh, and you'll return—that things will be the same. You made sure at every turn that I knew you loved playing games with my heart before breaking it apart. This time the joke is on you, because you lost someone true, someone who would have undoubtedly died for you, despite all you put me through. Now let me ask you again. Who do you think you are to try and have your cake and eat it too? I think you had your fun, but after a long run, it's finally done. Do you ultimately feel you've won, after what's been said and done? If I were you, I'd be left feeling blue and thinking of all the things I would undo. I would desire to turn back time and from the start say, "I choose you."

AS MAGNET AND METAL

I still think about you and the moments we shared. Though they were transient, they showed that you cared. I muse over the words we exchanged, the laughs we had every now and again. The stolen glances, the shameless stares, how we always found ourselves grouped in a pair. The reasons we would find to be side by side, how our desire to be together was hard to hide, and how my love for you took me like an ocean tide. Though this chronicle of my life can best be described as a roller-coaster ride, I can't quite say that I mind or that I don't often hit rewind and play back in my mind the memories of you that draw me back every time I consider letting go. My brain screams yes, but my heart says no. I care so much more than I let show, but surely you must know the effect you have on me, how a few of your words leave me smiling uncontrollably. Now I must confide, you've left me in a bit of a bind; common sense tells me I must let you go, yet my heart's investment in you steadily grows. Though countless times I've gotten over you, something's always drawn me back. Expertise in toying with my emotions is one thing you've never lacked. But don't think me bitter; I allowed it to be. If I am quite honest with myself, the fault lies partly with me and how, despite my better judgment, my heart goes back to you endlessly. Which then leaves me reminiscing and wondering what it is that I may be missing when you're not near and I can't feel your gaze, when you're not here and I can't see your face. I thought it would just be a phase and that I would move on. Yet you still set my heart ablaze and send my nerves into a craze; the feeling is not gone. I look back and smile. I know that it's real. I know what I feel and that it's reciprocated; but to what extent, I don't know. You're simply not clear in the messages you show. Today it's yes; tomorrow it's no; the next day it's maybe so. Therefore you can see where my confusion lies. When I'm ready to say goodbye, you suddenly say hi, then for my attention vie; consequently I sigh and wonder why this is what you decide to do. What do you mean? Yesterday you did not see me; now you're going out of your way to speak to me. This time, I'm not having it. I don't want to just let it be and make it seem like your indecision is consequence-free and that you can go hopping in and out of my life endlessly, because my heart's a given…yet I give in…to that smile that I adore and those eyes that make my heart soar…and it begins again: this push-and-pull dance of going back and forth, commenced by a glance that thereafter left me entranced.

NO LONGER A FOOL FOR YOU

I love you. I love getting lost in your eyes and consumed by your smile. I would happily drown in your dimples and die in your arms. I guess it's no secret now that I'm taken by your charms. Perhaps that's the reason I ignore the sounding alarms, and turn a blind eye to all of the harm that you've caused me, simply because you sometimes leave me feeling fuzzy and warm. Though more often than not, you leave me feeling torn. You're good, I must say, because more frequently these days, you play games with my heart yet somehow get me to stay. Every time I finally let go, you draw me back with the false hope that things will change, but instead, everything remains the same, and again and again I'm left feeling drained. I'm left feeling pained and slightly insane for deciding to believe you when you feigned that you'd changed. But again it was a game to get me to stay, and now I'm not sure exactly who is to blame. By now I know better, but somehow I allow my guards to come down when you come around and persistently seek my attention as though nothing has happened and act like I should be happy to see you, despite what you've put me through. I feel like a fool, because I thought that I knew how to walk away from something unhealthy, yet here

I am readily welcoming you with outstretched arms back into my heart, hoping for a fresh start, and finding myself mistaken for hoping in vain. They say we accept the love we think we deserve, which makes me wonder if I'm so insecure and unsure of myself that when you have the nerve to treat me as you do, I give you chance after chance, as though I have not learned from the past—but at last I remember that I have. It's just that each time I walk away, sure of the fact that I deserve better, you eventually or suddenly come my way and make sure that I remain tethered to you, though you know you have no intention of letting something substantial form and that you're just as lukewarm as before. All in all, yes, I'm often taken by your charms and at times imagine being wrapped in your arms, but I've come to the conclusion that I'm done with this confusion, and that this time I'm drawing the line and letting you know that it's time all this came to a close. I choose to let go. I wish you the best, but I've finally decided to put this to rest.

REMNANTS OF YESTERDAY

We could have been so happy if you would have just let us. It would have been so effortless, seamless, and continuous. I didn't really have expectations; I just wanted to be with you. My only desire was to be together, even just as friends, all through and through. I hardly understand your actions. At times you would greet me and speak to me, then incessantly pursue me, only to go right back to ignoring me or jumping at the opportunity to drive a dagger right through me. Honestly, what did you hope to achieve with the endless mixed messages you would constantly send? I just wanted it to end so that my aching heart could mend, but again and again when I would distance myself, you would reel me in, only to take my heart and shatter it for reasons unknown, and then decide that was the day you wanted to leave me alone. Quite often you left me in disbelief as to why you continuously went back and forth. I knew this treatment wasn't what I should have received and that sometimes you most likely talked to me because you were bored. My question was; if you were dissatisfied elsewhere, why wouldn't you just be with me? And if you truly cared, like you obviously seemed to, why didn't you have the courtesy to be consistent in treating me right—or leaving me entirely?

You know, I could hardly conceive the notion that you actually thought it was perfectly fine to hurt me then come back unapologetically and somehow think that I wouldn't mind or find it out of line, that I was supposed to just put it all behind. It really perplexed me that you thought you could just hop in and out of my life, return to retrieve me after leaving me reeling, only to take me on yet another emotional roller-coaster ride. I would proceed to ignore you, but then you would vie for my attention until the guard around my heart would subside. With hesitation I would let you inside my heart only for you to—right on cue—again break it apart. I didn't know what to make of this. Clearly you wanted me, yet simultaneously and unfortunately you seemed to enjoy spiting me, hurting me, and pushing me away until I truly wanted nothing to do with you and the games you repeatedly played. Oddly and inexplicably, though I no longer liked you, I somehow still loved you and, stranger still, actually cared about you. I tried to deny it. I didn't want to accept it, that I actually felt so strongly towards someone who regularly disregarded me and whose behavior was so hard to pardon. If you hadn't complicated things unnecessarily, we could have had something lovely, something substantial that would have undoubtedly withstood the test of time. Now instead we're left with the bittersweet memories that I've utilized to compose this rhyme.

MY HEART'S PREDICAMENT

Somehow I still love you, despite all that you've put me through. It makes no sense: I thought it would end, yet somehow it's continued. I doubt that I cross your mind as frequently as you cross mine, which irks me because if we had not crossed paths, I wouldn't be in this bind. I long to move on and leave what transpired between us behind. I just want these feelings gone and for this desire to subside. Yet I find myself increasingly gravitating towards thoughts of you and have to remind myself that in order to move forward I must forget you. It's honestly hard to put into words because it's perplexing and absurd. What we had can't even be described as substantial, which is why I've arrived at the conclusion that there must be more to this disillusionment. The moments we've shared have been few and far in between, but strangely sufficient in keeping you on my mind and in my heart, regardless of the time we've spent apart. It's increasingly bizarre that you're so far, yet I still see you each and every day in every way one can imagine. You couldn't fathom these strange happenings. I'm still grappling with the meaning of these mysterious occurrences and, of course, what prompted it all: our chance meeting. Could it be that indeed we're meant to be? That's what the signs suggest, or so it seems, because the distance between us has not caused this connection to dissolve. On the contrary, it's deepened it and created a puzzle I've not yet solved and left me questioning why most all my thoughts have been revolving around you, though I try without success to not let them to. I struggle to understand how these feelings still linger. We have hardly interacted, yet I've been unable to hinder my love from increasing instead of finally ceasing. What frustrates me is that I do and don't want to be yours. Although I do love you, I don't envision you as my always, not with the numerous doubts you've elicited and strange behavior you've exhibited. I thought you were different. You seemed like such a nice guy. I guess that was a lie, and that I should just try harder to put this behind. But you see, that's the thing I do through and through, but my mind constantly goes back to you. With great irritation I'll just have to accept that this is how things will be indefinitely. It's a shame 'cause I believed that this would actually work out. I was deceived; clearly I didn't know what I was talking about. All that this has amounted to is disappointment and heartbreak, and once again I'm left trying to make sense of these events. At the end of the day, I'd just like to gain closure on what's taken place, because I can't stand the thought of things staying the same and these loose ends remaining unknotted. Sometimes I even regret the day that we met, because the aftermath has had adverse effects on me. It's just that matters of the heart are hard. My brain says, "What are you doing? Do you like getting hurt?" Then my heart intercepts, saying, "Just give him another chance; it may be worth it." Then my brain interjects, saying, "You know he doesn't deserve it; things have only worsened." Needless to say, this leaves me stuck in between. Obviously I know it's long since been time to let go, and honestly I'm ready. But each time I do, something steadily pulls at my heart, making it hard to fully part. It's like something hits rewind in my mind, bringing me back to the time when there were more good times than bad, the time I was exceedingly glad when I saw or thought of you…unlike now, when the thoughts or memories of you are mostly shadowed by the great pain you've put me through. Despite all of this, I somehow still love you, though I've tried tirelessly to resist it. Unfortunately it may be this way indefinitely, but I'm no longer focusing on the negative. I have no control over what's already unfolded, but I do have a say in the decision I'm now making. I refuse to give you room to play me again. Not "someday" but *today* is when this comes to an end.

STUCK ON YOU

How is it that I still feel this way? When you stare deep into my eyes, it takes my breath away and transports me to an alternate place, that I wish existed in reality so I wouldn't have to dream about it and live a false fantasy. I tell myself it makes no sense for me to hold on to something so non concrete, but when you gaze into my eyes, I'm hypnotized, and my logic drifts away with the wind. When we maintain eye contact for an extended amount of time, all what I've tried to tell myself about how you've given me little to hope for is quickly forgotten, and I'm left longing for more than the few words we've exchanged in passing and laughs we've had every now and again. I tell myself there's no logic in holding on to something so inconsistent, but fleeting as the sweet moments we've shared have been, they've also been enough to keep me toughing out this struggle-love in hopes of it finally amounting to what we could clearly have so easily if you would come to your senses, stop pretending you don't feel the love you do, and just let our love flow, as opposed to turning everything into a needless battle. Sometimes I actually frustrate myself more than you do, because I know how you are, yet my heart refuses to let go. In my mind I obviously know that it's only a matter of time before you return to going back and forth, but the glimmers of hope you give me that this time you're finally ready to be different than you have been in the past—and, at last, commit to me—fool my heart into holding on despite all that's gone wrong between us because of what you've said and done. I don't know how I still love you and as much as I do. You've treated me badly and taken me for granted, yet a part of my heart still belongs to you. What I can't understand is that no matter what you've dragged me through, I've never been mad at you. I've felt hurt and betrayed but never angry with you. I've wished I could, because that would make it easier to see things objectively and finally let you go for good. Instead it seems that I only look at you through rose-colored glasses, which hinder me from seeing things as they are consistently. When you're playing your silly, spiteful games with my heart, the glasses come off—and with them the fog that always prevents me from moving on. But when you tender up and suddenly come towards me with all sorts of charm, I find it hard to keep up my guards, which I build higher and higher each time you leave me high and dry after hurting me, before trying to waltz back into my life like everything's fine and forgotten. When you smile and stare into my eyes, I'm unable to maintain my stony resolve; it immediately dissolves, and I sense cracks starting to form in the walls I thought were strong enough to resist you. The walls then go soft and crumble, leaving my heart exposed for you to most likely take it and break it again. I don't know why when it comes to you that my heart refuses to listen to reason. My brain doesn't tolerate a bit of your mistreatment; instead it urges my heart to learn from past experiences, but my heart won't have it and instead insists on holding on. Perhaps it's because you give me butterflies like no one else ever has, excite me with an intensity that I didn't know was possible, and because you've ignited a love for you so deep and profound that I would rather endure it than forfeit it, regardless of how strenuous it most often is. How is it that instead of being upset with you, I'm upset with myself? Instead of remembering all that you've put me through and using those memories to finally get over you, all I can think to myself is, "Girl, what's with you? Why do you continue to accept inconsistency, manipulation, and confusing mixed messages from him time and time again? Don't you think you deserve better than scraps and skinny love from someone who won't commit or at the very least have the courtesy to exit your life entirely? Yeah, every time he comes back into your life, you're always aloof and don't welcome him with open arms, but when he persists, the walls guarding your heart cease to exist, and there you are, ready to give him another chance once again." Somehow I don't hold anything against you; instead all I can do is think to myself, "You don't grow tired of heartache and frustration, do you? If so, why do you allow him one chance after the next, when you know he most likely is going to behave the same way as before?" My answer is a simple, "I don't know." What I do know is that I deserve far better than this, but the thing is…I just love him, even if I know that loving him comes with pain and having to defy the reason of my brain. If only this was a matter of logic and reasoning, then it would have been resolved ages ago, but it's not. It's a matter of the heart, and such matters are arduous, as you know. From a logical standpoint, of course I'm aware that this is not at all what I ought to be settling for, but it's as though there's some unseen force working behind the scenes to ensure that I'm always drawn back to you and eternally stuck on you, tiresome and cyclical as the situation may be. Unfortunately this isn't a matter of adding two and two and arriving at four: common sense seems to take a back seat when it comes to you and me. Instead what takes the lead is a heart set on holding on to a love that, although is so deep, is accompanied by instability. Another nonsensical aspect of our relationship, apart from my heart sort of accepting your mistreatment, is your overall behavior from nearly the very start. You clearly can't stay away from me or shake me, and we both know that no one else has the effect on you that I do. Since when are you shy or unable to find something to say? Yet when you're around me, you're tongue tied and frequently have to look away. When we're not in conversation and you're a short distance away, your eyes never leave me, yet you want to pretend that you can forget me and how you've felt from the first moment we met? I don't think so, and you always make it known when you inevitably make your way back to me without fail. So instead of playing games and hopping in and out of my life, the next time you return, why don't you stay and seek to make things right? So we can cultivate a healthy relationship, since you know it's only a matter of time before you once again realize that nothing and no one else inspire this undeniable love and interest within you like I do. Like metal to a magnet, you'll definitely be drawn back. So instead of wasting time by delaying, why don't you just remain true to your heart and be where you feel most loved? It's not as hard as you're making it out to be; you know no one loves you like me, and is as patient and forgiving with you, and I know this to be true because you don't treat anyone else as badly through and through. Yet here I am with my heart still fixed on you. I wish how you treated me could make me livid and see red, but instead the only red I see is the tint from the lenses of the rose-colored glasses I look at you through. There's simply no rhyme or reason to any of this; I only get skinny love from you yet hold on to it with such devotedness despite my better judgment, though it breaks my heart more and more each time I'm reminded that you still haven't changed. It doesn't make sense, but I'm never even upset with you, just myself once again when it turns out I only opened myself up to get gutted again. You don't make sense either. You go back and forth, complicating everything needlessly, when in reality you could just be with me or keep your distance permanently the next time you leave. But since you've shown that that's not possible, you could just let things flow naturally and stop fighting what you know you feel so deeply. I don't know what you think my expectations were after we met; they weren't grand, I didn't have any demands, I just wanted us together, even if that meant just being friends. Although it goes without saying that I was hoping we'd be something more, especially considering the ethereal beauty of our first meeting. It was truly surreal, which I know is part of the reason why I still hold on to us, because if that brief but enchanting moment was so impactful, then imagine how sublime a substantial relationship between you and I would be. You know this sentiment is reciprocated, which is part of your reason why you always come back to me. So for what reason are you so afraid? There's no pressure at all whatsoever; did you think that after we met, I was expecting a marriage proposal when we were only high school sophomores? I just wanted to be with you and hear about your day. I just wanted to love you and keep a smile on your face. There are few things I can think of that affect me like your smile; it gives me butterflies and makes my heart flutter. It warms me up inside and lights me up every time. It makes me sigh and smile simultaneously, and never ceases to make me weak. Even when I'm convinced that at last I've had it with you, I see it and my defenses go with the wind. And all I can think about is how tall, dark, and handsome you are, instead of how you've relentlessly played with my heart and played one mind game after the next. It perplexes me and somehow always results in me beating myself up for what you've done, because I know what to expect from you and that it's mostly trouble, which is why I put my guard up so you can't get through. Yet you always manage to at my expense, and then I'm left kicking myself for letting my walls down, somehow forgetting that it wasn't a conscious decision and instead was a direct result of your manipulation. Still, as I sit here aware of this, it pains and frustrates me, but I must admit to myself that still...I love you. It hurts, but I still love you. It doesn't make sense, but I guess that's just what unconditional love is. Time has proven to me that no matter what, I'll continue to love you for better or worse; in good times and bad, my love for you will endure. It doesn't make sense, but like I said: I guess that's just what unconditional love is. It's powerful and surpasses common sense, transgressions, and whatever you try to tell yourself in an attempt to get your heart to just let go, only to eventually discover that although you thought at last you had, that wasn't so, regardless of all that's happened in the past. I don't know how I still love you, despite what's transpired. I would think all that you've said and done would be substantial enough to erase my love for you, but that's just not true. Somehow my heart still holds on, painful as it may be, and with that devotion to you comes great inner conflict, because as I've mentioned, my brain urges me to let go, but my heart simply won't—not fully, at least. As I've previously said, I've gotten over you more times than I can count, but something always draws me back, and it can't just be my heart, because my heart has grown so tired of getting broken apart, which is why I wonder if it's something more, such as that unseen force I spoke of, strange as it may sound. I've never experienced a love like this; so deep, passionate, and long lasting, it's like nothing I've ever known. But on the flip side, since the nature of this love isn't conditional or fickle, for me it's also been painful, because it's ensured that although you've put me through so much, my love for you has endured, and despite my efforts to sever the tie, my heart's still tethered to yours.

A LETTER TO MY FOREVER
(DEAR FUTURE HUSBAND)

I want to trace along your strong jawline and feel your excitement rise as I lean in close and gaze into your eyes. I want to cover your beautiful ebony skin in infinite kisses and live at least five lifetimes so we can spend a couple like this. I want to gently caress your handsome face and lay in your warm embrace as our surroundings fade away. I want us to remain intertwined day after day and night after night, dedicating every moment to love. I want to feel your heartbeat against mine along with the warmth of your breath on my neck. I want to feel the tender pressure of your full lips against mine as they open and close in time to the rhythm of our passion. I want us to stare into each other's eyes until our heartbeats synchronize, reminding us of the time we met and how our breath caught in our chests as we stood frozen in time. Love of my life, I just want to watch you smile and spend every day by your side. I want to wake up to your beautiful face and fall asleep in your loving embrace, pressed against your broad chest and wrapped in what I can only describe as home: your arms. I want to give you my heart and endless affection and tell you the many reasons why I just love you. I want to feel your tender touch leave me with goosebumps and a headrush as I savor every second, because I honestly wonder if the time we spend together will ever feel as though it's enough. I want to give you every bit of my love, which only grows with each passing moment, and bestow you with more affection than anyone has ever known. I want to be yours and call you mine for the rest of time and beyond, if that's possible. I just want us together, forever and then some. Your smile alone makes my heart sore and soar, and as if it weren't catching enough on its own, the pairing with your dimples is more than I can handle, and your eyes…your piercing eyes, they simply take me to new heights. I can hardly describe how much I love you, but what I can say without hesitation is that I would die for you. I would lay down my life for the sake of you being able to continue living yours. I want to live with you and build with you, and for us to support one another as we work to achieve great feats. Along with this, I'd like us to enjoy the simple things, such as a quiet night spent outside under the cover of a blanket of stars, with me wrapped in your arms or you with your head on my chest. Just you and I, happy to be alive, if not for anything else but the pleasure of this experience. I'm so grateful for this love; there's no question as to whether it was sent from above. Something like this must have been divinely orchestrated, and what's better is that we met each other so young. I feel Heaven blessed when I consider that the rest of our lives together consist of many decades to come. My sweet love, what we have is second to none, I have no need for fantasies; our romance story is already like a dream, but far much better because it's reality. I never get used to how you make me feel. You smile and I melt immediately; you gaze into my eyes and I'm on cloud nine. The intensity of our chemistry never lessens; if anything, it steadily rises to the point where it's overwhelming. I would expect that with time, this thrill would subside a bit, but to my pleasant surprise, it's been quite the opposite. I always long for you, and you're constantly on my mind. I wonder if it's possible to ever get enough of you or if this deep desire will only continue to climb. I wouldn't mind trying to find out; after all, we do have time on our side. You know, you kind of drive me wild; I've never seen a man so fine. I still don't grow tired of admiring your beauty. You honestly never have an off day; it shocks me. I just love how you are, your easy-going demeanor, confidence, and effortless charm, but I think it's cute how I seem to disarm you, 'cause when you talk to me, all that goes with the wind. Suddenly Mr. Confident is laughing and looking away, struggling to maintain eye contact, and hardly finding the right words to say. It's okay; you know I feel the same way and that the feeling will always remain. There isn't an array of things we are assured of, but one thing you can always count on is my deep and unwavering love. Though everything around us may change, my love for you will never fade. I can hardly explain how much I love you. You've been my sunshine and the cause for some of my broadest smiles. The phrase "The best things in life are free" now has a deeper meaning to me, because there is truly nothing that can be purchased that I would rather have than this. There is nothing I would exchange for all that I've gained since the moment we first locked eyes. I love you more than life itself. Precious love of mine, what we have is one of a kind. Where can I begin in describing what our love has done for me? It's filled me with joy and employed feelings I had previously only dreamed of. It's given life to the concept of unconditional love, because I have, do, and will always love you, no matter what. I just want to hold your hand and walk side by side through life. I want to cuddle for hours and just enjoy each other's company, eventually fall asleep and wake up in each other's arms, face to face in a loving embrace. I want to squeeze your big, broad shoulders and run my hands over your beautiful frame, kiss all over your beautiful face, and stop to get a taste of your kissable lips as you take hold of my hips, run one hand up my waist, and pull me closer, as we let go and let love take control. When the desire has been quenched and we lay back to rest intertwined somewhere between space and time, I want us to remain just as connected as we were a moment ago and be one in mind, body, and soul, only growing closer with each passing second and continually vibrating on the same wavelength. As we gaze into each other's eyes and our heartbeats begin to synchronize, I want you to be reminded that in you a part of me lies, as you in I. Our love is timeless; it will always last, even as the seasons pass. I want you to know that with me, you can always be vulnerable; I'll never shy away when you cry or feel uncomfortable when you show emotion. I welcome your heartfelt expressions telling of how you really feel. I encourage you to be free whenever you confide in me. Our relationship is not just one-dimensional; it's layered and multifaceted, which is why I cherish it that much more. Because along with the passionate, romantic aspect of it, we're best friends till the end and then some. We're lifelong allies through every low and every high. We can be each other's source of support and encouragement through all of life's trials. Come what may, I'll always be there; you can count on me because you know I'm yours. There's no one else I'd rather weather a storm with: I'm safe in the knowledge that it won't tear us apart; it could only strengthen our love and bring us closer together. You can always rely on me, that goes without question. I'll always abide with you, no matter the situation. You don't know how much I love you. You smile at me and my heart sings. Despite our differences, we're kindred spirits, and my love for you is soul deep. Your eyes give me a natural high, and your presence still gives me butterflies. When I envision my forever, it's you that I picture. Whether it's winter or summer, autumn or spring, there is no one I'd rather spend my life with. I want to give you all of the happiness and laughter you've gifted me with and be your constant source of encouragement and comfort. I want to be the reason your life flows with more ease and the one who lets you know that you're never alone. You don't have to worry about my loyalty: you know that you're my one and only for the rest of eternity. I'm unquestionably set on just us being together, making sweet memories and endless love, building castles in the sky, and climbing higher side by side. I love you. I want to be yours for all time and call you mine for the rest of our lives.

AFRAID TO LOVE
BECAUSE OF YOU

They say it's better to have loved and lost than to have never loved at all. But when I think of you, I wonder how true this is, because loving you has caused me so much sorrow. You're the reason that when a guy shows me time after time that he has nothing but the best intentions, I can't help but second guess him and question whether his seemingly genuine words and behavior are just a guise to hide his true nature. Because if one were to ask someone to describe you, they would say the nicest things, but between you and I, we know there's another side to you that you would rather stay masked. A side that allowed you to play games with my mind, take me on one emotional roller-coaster ride after the next, spite me left and right—although it was always unprovoked and you know that—shatter my heart, ice me out for a while, then act like nothing happened when you would try to talk to me again. You're the reason that when I'm presented with the possibility of a healthy relationship, I have quite a bit of doubt, because I can't help but think of the times that are too many to count where you intentionally toyed with my heart, broke it apart, and treated me unkindly at times with the hope of riling me up, only to be met with the disappointment of not being able to get a reaction out of me. You're the reason that when I find myself catching feelings, anxiety sets in, and I wonder how long it'll be before he has me reeling. You're the reason that I no longer look forward to falling in love again, for fear of the pain, anguish, and senseless games that may follow. I've even been feeling increasingly jaded towards romance; me: a hopeless romantic. I could have never imagined that I would develop a cynical view toward romantic relationships. You're the reason I'm afraid to love, because you've shown me that no matter how much, how truly, how unconditionally, and how deeply you love someone, it may not be enough to prompt them to open their eyes, realize how good they have it, and treat you right. This has been a sad discovery, but I guess it was necessary. I just wish I could hold on to this lesson alone and better release this stress I now associate with relationships. Your hurtful actions have really had a lasting impact that I've not yet been able to get past. I want to trust, but I struggle to let my heart reopen. I constantly wonder if I'm just setting myself up to get my heart shredded again. You're the reason that I've gone from considering all that could go right to counting all the possible cons and wondering how long it'll be before giving him a chance backfires and leaves me feeling foolish for believing that things could have actually worked out differently. You're the reason that when a guy proves to be perfect on paper, I still have trouble trusting whether things will unravel differently than they have with you. I want to move forward with an open heart and embrace love when it finds me, but each time it does, I find myself wanting to run, because at least when I'm on my own, I don't get my heart broken. All the while, I wonder whether I'm guarding my heart to the point that I just might be blocking a blessing waiting to be received. I want to let go of the past and all that's happened between us, but I worry if I let my guard down and open my heart, I'll only find out what I feared: that what appeared to be perfect was indeed too good to be true. In all honesty, it's not like you don't possess good qualities. In truth there are numerous traits that I admire in you, which is why I held on for far longer than I should have and regrettably decided to overlook the red flags. Because in my mind at the time, I believed that what I admired could override what I disliked. Clearly I was really misguided, which is why ever since I've had a great sense of trepidation, even when a guy seems to be totally genuine. I worry time will reveal that he is quite the opposite and that, like you, he just likes playing games, leaving my head spinning, then acting like nothing's the matter. You're the reason I teeter back and forth in between letting go of my doubts— that stem from my memories with you—and anticipating how all will go wrong before I'm given a sign that anything is amiss. Because of you when things are going smoothly, I start to have doubts and wonder how long it'll be before everything goes south. It's annoying because before I knew you, I never entertained such negative trains of thought. Now when everything is seemingly so good, I can't help but think it's because there's something I've overlooked. I can't help but wonder if there's a major deal breaker that I've refused to reconcile myself with because reality may be less attractive than the fantasy I'd rather upkeep. These days, when a new guy starts to talk to me, I nearly get anxiety as I recall all that you've put me through and worry it'll only be more of the same but with someone new. I try and try to let go of the lie that a happy, healthy relationship can't possibly be mine and that I can't actually end up with a man who doesn't drain, stress, and confuse me, take and take, yet only give me heart and headaches. But it's a difficult lie to unlearn, since it's what I've grown so accustomed to during the time that I've known you. I greatly desire to only hold on to the lessons I've learned from this experience, but it's much easier said than done. Subconsciously I fear that if I stop being so closed off, then I'll only open myself up to immense heartache again, conclude that it was a mistake, and brim with disappointment. You're the reason I don't want to open up to love again. I know it could be well worthwhile, like a sweet dream realized. However, I'm also wary that instead it could prove to be a nightmare, which is why I feel stuck in between my desire to overly guard my heart from more harm and my longing to let go of the old to allow what may be a blessing to unfold. You're the reason I'm afraid to love, and now overly guard my heart. You're the reason I put several walls up and consider running from something good almost as soon as I see it approaching. You're the reason I have trouble trusting, even when I'm given no reason to have questions. You're the reason I avoid things having to do with romance, because they remind me of how badly you toyed with me in the past. But you know what? I'm done being closed off for fear of only the worst unfolding. I'm no longer writing off what I used to dream of due to what I've endured with you. Though you've dragged me through so much and robbed me of nearly all of my optimism, I'm not going to worsen the situation by vowing never to love. Over time I learned to have trust issues and expect various versions of what you put me through, but this tiresome cycle of expecting the worst while halfheartedly hoping for the best has run its course. I'm not going to start searching for or chasing down love, but in good time, when it finds me, I'll no longer feel inclined to run.

A LETTER FROM YOURS TRULY

When I think back on things, it honestly shocks me that I thought the fault was partially my own, in regards to how you mistreated me. I really wasn't seeing clearly; if I had, I would have known that you were playing mind games. Again and again you hurt and mislead me into thinking that things would be different; then you would return, pretend that nothing had happened, and the tiresome cycle would commence once more. I sometimes wondered if you got bored with the same things occurring repeatedly, on a loop, nothing new, no progression, only stagnation and frustration, when things could have been so simple and seamless between us. I can hardly reconcile myself with the fact that each time you came back, you would act as though everything was fine, blind to the pain you had inflicted, the mistakes you had made, and the wounds they had induced. Then somehow you managed to bring down my guards, and like a fool I allowed you back into my heart. I chided myself when you ended up hurting me again, as I struggled to discover why I hadn't sided with common sense. Of course I knew that I should have expressed that I'd rather you left me alone or, at the very least, stop playing games with me. Yet for some reason—and I wasn't sure why—I couldn't bring myself to, or so it seemed. What I neglected to acknowledge is that you never allowed that opportunity to arise. Each time you would spite or covertly insult me; it was always in public, so I couldn't say anything without taking the risk of looking crazy or touchy. You were crafty. Every time it was like you contrived a plan that would do as much damage as you could manage, in a way that was entirely underhanded, so that only I would get the malicious message you were sending and you would still seem nice to the public eye. Even with all this, I often went back and forth; most of the time, I was over you, but deep within my core, there was something that prevented me from fully closing that door, something that stopped me from no longer being yours to toy with whenever you got bored only for you to soon ignore me again like times before. It's as though there was a chord I couldn't cut, though I tried without any luck. This must have somewhat been the case for you as well, because even though you tried to deny how you truly felt inside, it was written plainly in your eyes and confirmed each time you returned. Yet instead of attempting to make things move forward, you would start from where you left off and use the same half hearted approach. It's as though you wanted me to go, "Oh my goodness! He's talking to me again!"—profess my love and forget all that you'd said and done. When that wouldn't happen, you would get upset and senselessly seek an enemy in me, absent-minded of the fact that I was the one constantly on the receiving end of your callous words and actions; yet still I never returned the ill treatment you sent me. I couldn't understand how you had feelings for me yet simultaneously were at war with me, of all people. Could you not recall who endlessly made things harder than they needed to be? Couldn't you see that I never did a thing to provoke you, despite that being what you regularly did to me? Then ironically you would start to resent me, maybe because you hated that you loved me, and possibly because you felt guilty for treating me badly and speaking to me rashly. Or perhaps it was due to you being annoyed that you were unable to get me to react. Whatever the reason, it was uncalled for. You were totally out of line, especially when you would come back and never attempt to make things right. There were many wrongs to be rectified. Was I just supposed to set them aside? Even the time you pretended you'd forgotten me, just to play with my mind, and then—you guessed it—tried to talk to me like things were fine? What about the time you saw me walking by, then stopped to pointedly look in my eyes, then turn to your girlfriend, telling her you love her with a sly smile on your face, simply for the sake of stabbing my heart with a dagger in the form of your affection towards her. What about when you asked me my name, as though you didn't already know it, and had me questioning whether I was sane or if I had in fact imagined what happened between us, such as the day we met and the intensity we felt. You had me honestly wondering whether it was all in my head. Was I supposed to forget this and the unnecessity of it, when instead you could have left me alone, as opposed to putting your efforts towards bringing me low? What about your cutting words; should I have forgotten them too? What always made it worse is that you smiled as you spoke them; it was actually funny to you. What about the careless things you said? While they weren't as cold and calculated as a couple of the things previously mentioned, they showed your disregard towards me, which, in a way, stung just as much as when you would intentionally spite me. Need I remind you of the time when you said you didn't love me, that it was just lust? Once again, it was so unnecessary, but you just couldn't pass up the opportunity to gut me needlessly, like I was your enemy. How couldn't you know that I was on your side, that if you would have let me I would have been your closest ally, in every low and every high, someone to confide in without fear of judgment. Instead of taking advantage of this, you took the endless chances I gave you for granted. Believe it or not, none of this is what pained me the most. What hurt me the worst were the times when you looked past me like I didn't exist as resentment emanated from you. It was heartbreaking and devastating to think that someone I loved so dearly suddenly and inexplicably hated me so seriously. Was all this and more what I should have immediately tossed out the door when you would come waltzing back into my life after having said or done something that purposely cut like a knife? You would deliberately push me away and then be surprised when that was where I wanted to stay. There was no end to the questions you elicited, which reminded me of a quote I once read; it goes something like this: "You don't realize how much you love someone or how much peace you have without them until they're gone." It may gladden and sadden you to hear this, but you were the first one to come to mind. Though most of the time I was over you and past what I thought we could have had, at times my thoughts gravitated towards you and my heart longed for you like mad. On the other hand, the absence of your presence granted me so much peace. So while at first I would feel sad when you would hop back out of my life, it swiftly turned to relief. There was a time when I thought I could give you one last chance, and with all things considered, we could still rekindle the flame that burned in our hearts. The more I pondered the past, I couldn't get past the fact that you always placed me last. If you had chased just one other, sincerely apologized, explained how you had made a mistake, you didn't know what you were thinking, and that you'd had a lapse in judgment, you would have gotten me to understand. Here's the thing: you knew exactly what you were doing, and there wasn't just one. There were a ton of others you were pursuing, and all the while, you had the audacity to continually come back to me and expect me to gladly allow it to be. Sadly my unconditional love for you caused me to tolerate a lot in the past, but things have changed. I'm done with this tiresome game. I've waited too long, which has given me time to contemplate and remember all that I was dragged through needlessly. You caused the loss of quite a bit of my peace and self-esteem. Innumerable times you made me feel not good enough, which is especially tough to forget, more so when I pair it with everything else that I've mentioned. The pettiness I can put out of my mind, but what I can't push aside is that you made me feel inferior. From the exterior, I would not let on how greatly you had pained me or how deep the wounds had gone, but internally you'd gutted me and directly taken a shot at my self-esteem, which helps make sense as to why my heart would defy my mind, and despite my better judgment, I would think we could give things another try. Because over time I had lost sense of some of my worth, from frequently being made to feel like dirt, from being fed bread crumbs as I was walking away so you could make sure that yours I would stay, from being gaslighted and spited, then surprised when out of the blue you would get nice again. The many slights I can put aside, but the more that I think about it, I can't push aside the time you pretended you'd forgotten me. It was something I tried to forget quickly for the sake of my sanity, but I can't let it be water under the bridge. You made me feel unhinged, and that was your intention. You stared me down with a gleam in your eyes, and that same sly smile spread broadly across your face, so much so that I had to look away. You nearly had me in tears; I couldn't believe my ears. Was I really hearing correctly? Was this actually happening? Were you trying to deny knowing me simply for the sake of hurting me, once again with no provocation, or had you honestly forgotten me? I wasn't sure which was worse, the thought of you putting effort towards hurting me so thoroughly or the fact that you had actually forgotten me. A thousand thoughts raced through my brain before I came to the conclusion that this was another one of your games. Just like times before this was a ploy to toy with and bruise me for your own delight and amusement. To tell you the truth, I never took you for a cunning one, but I certainly should've. This wasn't the first time you delivered a verbal gut punch so furtively and nonchalantly so that not one person would perceive the other meaning in your words except me. What I couldn't discern is why you yearned to hurt me; you wanted so much to crush me when I had literally done nothing. I couldn't see why you were full of glee, when there was not one time I treated you as you treated me. At that moment I saw this incident as the last straw. Once again you showed me that you could actually gain pleasure from taking measures to hurt me, which is something I couldn't take lightly; then unsurprisingly you tried to talk to me like things were fine. There was never an apology, and clearly your heart was not contrite, yet somehow you succeeded in slithering your way back into my life. So you can see why I've rebuilt the walls guarding my heart, ensured their security and manufactured them five times as high, so that if you try to come back into my life to beguile me again, you'll find that what once worked no longer has the same effect. If you try to slide through all smooth and confident, you'll find that I'm doing just fine without you, that I don't pine for you, that I'm thriving and new. For gone is the girl who needed higher self-worth, who accepted scraps and crumbs, knowing she shouldn't have and that it was dumb. I now stand in her place, and I must let you know: it's time that I say what I should have long ago. Never again will I let you try to grind me to dust, then turn around and charm me as you expect to be welcomed by my open arms and unguarded heart. Those days are gone: a new dawn has broken, and I'm done being conned. If you think that I'm kidding, then you are wrong. At last I'm leaving what once was in the past, where it belongs.

DON'T YOU DARE

In case you were considering walking back into my life after all
you've put me through one last time, I want you to know that,
finally, you're not welcome. You've played endless games with
my heart and my brain, caused me to feel insane, emotionally
unstable and, through the control you managed to gain over
me, led me to doubt reality and my very own memories. I
know in the past I granted countless allowances for your steadily worsening maltreatment towards me, but this time things
are different. I'm finally done being toyed with and torn up.
Over time I unfortunately grew resigned to this, accepting that
it's simply the way it must be; you treat me badly, and I just
have to tell myself it is what it is. Consequently I lost so much
self-esteem, because I thought that surely I must have brought
it upon myself. I learned to accept such great mistreatment and
dutifully take the blame. It still doesn't make sense, because not
once have I ever been unkind to you or dared to reciprocate
your deeply wounding mistreatment; instead I was overly forgiving. Even as things progressively got worse and I was more
and more hesitant in trusting you with my heart, I continued
to let it remain yours. What further grieves me is that the more
I ponder all this, the more I realize that I didn't deserve any of

it. Still as I write this, I'm not confident in what I say, because after years of enduring the calculated games you played with my heart and my brain, I still struggle to decipher between what you lead me to believe and reality. It's confounding because I try to tell myself that I haven't treated you or anyone else like this; therefore it's entirely unfit for me to be so badly treated, but I can't completely make this bit really stick. I figure since it happened and I accepted it, then it must be the normal order of things, and therefore I have no right to say this because it's just the way things are and it's up to me to simply accept it. I'm still not speaking freely, partially because I feel I'm being dramatic, since, after all, it could have been worse. But how else can I honestly feel when you seriously treated me badly? The other reason I feel I'm restricting myself as I speak is because all of this is what I've thoroughly grown used to, so I still grapple with being fully convicted that I deserve anything different. How could I be able to see things clearly when you held my heart, and with it the ability to crush me as you have so much of my self-esteem. I've said it before that you stole my heart, and now I've discovered that that's not all you took from me. You also robbed me of the ability to consistently see things clearly. As I write this, recalling all that you've painfully and undeservingly dragged me through over the years, I still feel bound by inhibitions to filter and water down what I say, because truly you've left me feeling unworthy of anything better than this. You've also filled me with doubt that a healthy relationship based on love, kindness, and respect could actually exist for me; instead I most always feel that in numerous aspects of it I'll most certainly be taking a loss and will just have to accept that that's just the way things go—because with you, that's now all I know. Gone are the days when I thought of you fondly and held any hope that we could possibly mend our relationship. Now the thought of you gives me anxiety, and all I can think is that I want nothing to do with you. Can you honestly blame me, considering how you've treated me? Because in all of this, I've done my best to be my best, but unfortunately it's never been enough. I've treated you with nothing but love and acceptance, contrary to what one would expect. The expected reaction for me to have in response to how you've brought me down and sought to rile me up, when all you were ever met with was love, is for me to serve you what you deserve, which is the same ill treatment you dished out to me. But I never did; instead I continued to love you and try my best to make things work. I've said it before, and I'm saying it again: my relationship with you has had a lasting adverse impact on me. Because even as I try to remind myself of all this—that it wasn't my fault, that I do deserve better, and that relationships don't necessarily consist of excess pain, confusion, and manipulation—up until this point I've been unable to shake this mind frame, despite my efforts to reason with myself. To my detriment, I am of the persuasion that sooner or later in a relationship, it will be laden with pain and emotional upheavals and leave me feeling insane for two reasons: the first being from your deliberate efforts to make me feel unhinged, and the other being from loving you so devotedly though you've treated me so badly. I ask myself why I've loved you so much, and I don't have a definitive answer. I know it's partially due to the spell I fell under immediately upon meeting you, which had me holding on to hope that things would soon return to how beautiful they were in those first moments between us. It's also partially due to how I grew used to being fed bread crumbs. Skinny love is all I've known from you, so it's what I held on to in hopes of it blossoming into something more substantial, as I also hoped that you would come to your senses and just start treating me well. I knew it was within your capacity, considering how very well you treated everyone else, whereas with me you played one game after the next for your own nonsensical amusement. What's even more perplexing is that I could never bring myself to be upset with you; instead I somehow always found a reason to blame myself. I would kick myself for not being more resolute in my attempts of resisting your charms, but regardless of how hard I tried, you were always able to find a way to make sure I remained yours and tied to you when I so longed to just be done with you. My relationship with you has been so conflicting and so vexing. You treated me so badly, yet I still loved you. I loved you more than life itself and kept you in my prayers. I used to thank the Most High for blessing me with the love of my life despite the hell you dragged me through. And you know very well what I'm referring to: not just your callous and careless, calculated, and heartless behavior but that devilish scheme you devised to ensure that I had to reach out to you despite not at all wanting to. You actually had the audacity to hurl me into a horrid situation in which my free will was so forcefully stolen from me. I'm not gonna bother to go into the details of it here because it's far too insane to put down on paper—plus you already know what I'm talking about. But do you know that you thoroughly robbed me of so much peace and that I could hardly sleep for months because of that garbage you sent my way when you could have more easily sent me a message expressing how you felt? Honestly, what's wrong with you? You had me quite literally living a nightmare, because you refused to be man enough to take the risk of being rightfully rejected, even though you know all too well that I was overly forgiving through all of what you put me through. So why did you think that I would be anything but understanding towards you this time, though we both know you don't deserve it? How could you treat me so badly, when you know you've never been met with such understanding, like you have with me? I loved you at your worst, and instead of being appreciative, you took it for granted and caused me more problems. Why are you like this? It's like you truly don't like nice things. Your cold attitude used to break my heart, but now I've grown so grateful for all of the times you shoved me away, creating a great gap between us that I don't ever want to lessen. I'm embarrassed to admit it, but it wasn't even your mistreatment that solidified my no longer wanting to be with you at the time when I was still going back and forth. Your cowardice and weakness when you did whatever it is that you did to get me to send you that message against my will and then all of that garbage that followed was the final nail in the coffin, since then I could never look at you in the same way. 'Cause honestly, how could you do that to me, someone you supposedly loved so deeply? Unfortunately with time, my love for you overrode the agony of what you dragged me through, and again I was ready to give you one last chance. But thankfully I opened my eyes and let go of what I thought was mine: a future with you and what I falsely believed was the love of a lifetime. My, was I living a lie. Another thing I've grown so grateful for is that it's been forever since we last saw each other. I've gotten the opportunity to think clearly and see things as they are, without you around muddling my judgment with your charms and playing one cunning game after the next with my heart. I know earlier I said I wasn't sure as to whether I deserved the ill treatment I received from you and that I was writing with hesitation because I was still filled with inhibitions. But some time has elapsed since I began this address, and since then I've been reunited with my common sense. I no longer wonder about things I used to be unsure of because of you, such as my memories; whether I can be in a relationship based on love, kindness, and respect; and if I did one thing to deserve even a bit of your mistreatment. I know without question I didn't. For the record, since you master manipulators love to work your magic by first seeking to piece apart someone's self-esteem, I'll have you know that although you were able to wreck much of mine temporarily through your skillful tactics and mind games, it's now higher than before you came along seeking to wreak havoc in my life for your own senseless gain. So if you think that you can try to slither back into my life, charm me, and possibly feed me lies so that you can take me on yet another emotional roller-coaster ride and have me once again wondering if I'm losing my mind, you better think twice. I'm no longer interested. I don't want or need your love, and I have no desire at all whatsoever for us to rekindle the fire that once burned. The past is the past, and I want no part of you at last. I don't want your lies or manipulation, your skinny love or games. I don't want my time wasted, your indecision, or you causing me to question whether I'm sane. You were a fool to let me get away, and I wouldn't have it any other way. You know very well no one else has ever shown you such love, kindness, forgiveness, and patience, and all you knew how to do was run from the one person who saw all your flaws and instead met you with love and acceptance. I'm glad I never chased you, or any guy for that matter, lest this tiresome cycle have been needlessly extended. I just wish you hadn't gone back and forth a million times between pushing me away and chasing me. It would have made everything much easier, but sadly you were always a fan of complicating things unnecessarily, as opposed to letting what would have obviously flown naturally take its course. I'm not exactly sure what your plans are for the future, but just know that I won't be a part of yours. I'm now in a healthy headspace and I know what I deserve, and it's certainly not whatever you have to offer. So if you think that you can walk back into my life claiming that you've changed and ask for one last chance, you should know that I'm not having it. I want nothing to do with you. You're no longer welcome, so forget whatever funny ideas you have about making your way back towards me. I'm done with you, so don't you dare.

WELL WISHES

This may come as a surprise to you, but I actually wish you well. You've put me through all sorts over the years, but I guess this is a testament as to what true love really does: it endures. Yes, I hope that you've learned your lessons in regards to all that you needlessly dragged me through. But I can honestly say that despite what's been said and done, I wish you nothing but great prosperity and the best of luck. I've made my peace with the past and that has allowed me to really consider what I've learned about love just from experiencing us. I've learned that, truly, love is patient and love is kind, despite events that may have transpired. Because the love I have for you, while no longer romantic, has somehow lasted despite the past, and sincerely cares to see you succeed, and even cares for your well-being. I'm almost surprised, but not entirely, because that's just how love is: it's the most beautiful force in the universe and can create unbelievable realities. I remember once upon a time when I began to get past what you had put me through, I wished you well in life but trouble in the area of love. That's no longer the case, and it's long since been this way: I even wish you well when it comes to love and romance. When you do happen to find love, I hope that you don't repeat the same mistakes that you did with me. I hope that all goes smoothly and that you both make each other happy. It's been a long while since we last spoke, and who knows when the next time will be. Whenever that is, I hope to find that life's been treating you right and even that you're thriving. Even though I no longer look at you through rose-colored glasses, I don't get upset, either, when you happen to come to mind. Now I think of you as someone whose path fatefully converged with mine in order to learn essential life lessons. One thing I definitely gained from this is the understanding that I don't need someone to complete me as I once believed. I am whole and complete as I am. In due time, when I find the right man, I won't see him as the missing part of me that I've always needed in order to feel complete but rather someone who beautifully complements my life as I would like to complement his. I've also learned to no longer hold on to skinny love. If someone shows me that he's only partially in, then I want no part of him. I'm grateful for these lessons and that I learned them at this time, so that none of my energy is spent on this sort of frustration later in life. I'm grateful for the wisdom that I've gained from our relationship, and I hope that you've gained some wisdom as well. We've had our highs and lows, and there was a time that you had me wishing I'd never known you. But like I said: I'm at peace with what's unraveled, and sincerely I wish you well. Take care and stay blessed.

LOW NOTE

You know, you really disappointed me, man. You were like a mentor to me and one of my favorite teachers; I even considered you to be a friend. But I guess your mind was always elsewhere, and not at all where it should have been. I don't know what your thought process was for you to think that I would be flattered by harassment, but it's clear we weren't on the same page, and it's a shame that I had to find out through your unwanted advances. I'm still surprised that's where your mind was, considering our difference in age. The gap could make you my grandfather, but to you that wasn't a bother. I still can't wrap my mind around the fact that you weren't put off by me being in my late teens and barely in my twenties during the time that you knew me. To any reasonable person, that would have been a cause to keep off. But to you it seemed like nothing. In case you were confused, I was never amused by your unwanted flirtations; I simply wasn't sure how to react. So I thought if I ignored you, you would get a clue and understand that I was in no way interested. Unfortunately you didn't perceive the obvious, or you decided to mistake my discomfort and shyness for interest. In case you weren't sure about what was plain as day: no, I didn't appreciate your inappropriate behavior; I just tried to shrug it off, telling myself that it could be worse. It's only when I stopped to ponder what I would consider it to be if it happened to someone else— and without a doubt I would say it's harassment. Everything from the strange things you would say every now and again to how you would sometimes get too touchy for no reason. To my disappointment and shock, you never saw the error of your ways until one day when you really went over the top by trying to kiss me against my will. I can't comprehend what possessed you in order for you to grab hold of me so forcefully and try to pull me in, causing me to put my hands up in between us as I turned away exclaiming, "No!" How could you not know what was so clear to see: that I was not interested in the least? It wasn't until then that you seemed to get that, after all, I wasn't interested. Yeah, you apologized in that one instance, but I highly doubt you wouldn't repeat a similar offense. I didn't want to accept that your intentions weren't the best. But the more I thought about it and the inappropriate things you've said in passing, it's what I've had to come to terms with to my disgust and disappointment. I can't help but shake my head when I reflect on how things are now, considering that I really did think of you as a mentor and a friend. With that said, I'll go ahead and wrap, since I've written what I wanted you to know. It's just too bad that things have ended on a low note.

DEAR MCKARTNEY

Dear McKartney, I'm sorry. I know it's been, like, fifteen years, and you've either forgotten—as I hope you have—or don't care to hear it, but I still thought I should express my heartfelt and honest apologies. There is no excuse for my mistreating you: it was a stupid thing to do, and I wish I had thought it through instead of being an idiot kid who decided to act on minor irritations. I wish I had stopped to think of how I would feel if I were in your position. It doesn't matter that I found you annoying; there is a manner in which I should have nicely expressed how I felt about how you would sometimes act out. But unfortunately I decided to forfeit kindness, and my silly first-grade brain decided to act on impulse, which resulted in me being mean. I know I was only seven and proper reasoning hadn't quite set in, but I don't want to blame my mistakes on age. I knew enough to do the right thing, and that's the kind thing, which would have been to ask myself how I would have felt if I were to be treated the same way. Sadly I didn't, and I've regretted it ever since, and honestly after all these years I'm still heartbroken over it. But that's the price I'll have to pay for my foolishness; I just hope you can find it in your heart to grant me forgiveness. I hope it makes you feel better to know that even though it was ages ago, I still feel terrible. I was so wrong and I'm so sorry. I truly wanted to apologize before the school year ended, but I was too much of a coward, and then the next thing I knew, the school year was through and I had lost my chance to rectify my wrongs. All in all I want you to know that I'm so sorry. I wish you the absolute best, and I hope this finds you doing very well.

DEAR DAVID

Dear David, you're disgusting and cowardly. You're unworthy of the name your parents gave you. You preyed on a teenage girl then turned around and tried to blame her for it. You even tried to blame God; I'm appalled at the thought of it. The mental gymnastics you performed in your convoluted brain must have been insane for you to have rationed out your actions and think that someone other than yourself was to blame. You somehow came to the conclusion that you were not at fault, that a higher force placed me in your life for your own sick and selfish desire. When that proved to be too much of a stretch for even your clearly warped mind, you then attempted to point a finger at me, instead of taking an honest look at yourself and shifting the blame back to where it should have been. One would think that someone who bears your name would be brave, courageous, and ready to take a situation such as this and boldly say they were wrong for their many and reprehensible mistakes—especially at your age— but in your case they would be mistaken. You did quite the opposite. Countless times you made obviously unwanted advances; I would shrug it off nervously, but I guess you somehow took it as flirting. Did it seem like I enjoyed it when you would stand too close, causing me to take several steps back only for you to follow? What about when there was no longer room to move back—was I not clearly uncomfortable as you would choose to ignore social cues and close the already minuscule gap? Did I seem thrilled when you would leer at me with your mouth quite literally agape? Because in reality you gave me chills down my spine and my neck's nape. Your behavior was abhorrent, but your sickness made you blind to this; otherwise you would have seen that you clearly gave me anxiety. Much of the time when you looked at me, it was as though you saw something to eat. You entirely resembled a predator drooling over meat, as it anticipated sinking its teeth into what it falsely perceived as its treat. For this reason among others, I made sure to keep my distance. I avoided you like the plague that you were, but it didn't stop your persistence. You continued to pursue me, and I obviously resisted. How were you so oblivious to how inappropriate this was? Did you think that I was nervous because I liked you back? I was really uneasy because you made me feel queasy. Did you think I would smile because I was happy to speak to you? I was simply trying to be nice; I didn't want to seem impolite, but I guess your twisted mind took this as an invite despite the frightfully obvious signs that your flattery didn't sit right with me. If your reasoning had been logical, you would have easily distinguished the difference between my normal attempt at being cordial and what you perceived as mutual attraction. How didn't you see what was plain as day? I stayed away from you and declined every invitation of yours to be anywhere you were. What possessed you into believing that your behavior was anything but egregious? Your unwavering stare was enough to make me feel like throwing up. It made me sick to think of the noxious thoughts that must have run through your putrid mind, more so now when I look back on that time. Just a few short years older, yet I see that I was a child and that you were so vile and serpentine in your actions that you actually acted as you did, then somehow found the audacity to turn things around and lead me to believe that the fault was mine. I was blind to the truth, and you certainly were too. You fully pulled the wool over my eyes and likely fed yourself some grandiose lie to try and justify what clearly was not right. I cannot begin to imagine what you could have possibly said to yourself, for your tasteless advances to actually make sense in your head. Which is why I really need answers, because I have struggled to decipher how you a youth pastor preyed on an underaged girl—faulted her for it—yet you were able to face yourself day after day, put up a false facade that all was okay and walk around like you weren't making many dangerous mistakes, while continually pursuing me despite my endless efforts to keep you at bay. I hardly know what to say or make of this. I'm at a loss for words. What's worse is that this occurred in church. All I can think is that you must have been sick. Were you so taken by your illness that you forgot what you claimed to be? A counselor of young souls, someone who should have led with integrity—but instead you proved to be a wolf in sheep's clothes. You used your position as a means for concealment of your gross violation of decent and proper conduct. Were you never overwhelmed with cognitive dissonance at any one point or time? Because it bewilders me to consider that you would actually gather biblical speaking points to relate to us while simultaneously chasing me and trying to find ways to be alone with me. It's so disgusting that it's almost funny. Except that it's not, because there is no humor to be found in your serious and ridiculous, ironic misconduct. I remember one time when you tried to teach about judgment and how people like to say, "Only God can judge me." You said that was all wrong because we should all judge each other righteously, which begs the question: Did you really think you had any place to speak about righteous judgment when you yourself clearly lacked a moral compass? What business did you have to inspect a speck in someone's eye when you were so blind to the plank in your own; your behavior could not be condoned, it was predatory to a tee, and if you beg to differ, consider how you would feel if some creep behaved the same way towards your daughter as you did me. It sickens me to think of it, and more so because as a whole so-called grown man who calls himself a pastor, you refused to own your own faults. I will admit there was one time, one single time before your behavior became out of line and I realized that your intentions weren't the best, to say the absolute least, when I behaved in a way that I shouldn't have. And wish that I could take back, one reason being because I was obviously wrong and the other reason being so that you would have no chance to claim an excuse for all that ensued. During that isolated incident that I'm referring to, you were tongue tied while trying to talk to me, so foolishly I decided to play it up, simply for the sake of gassing myself up, by seeing if I could really get you all jumbled up. But rapidly after that I regretted my lapse in judgment and immediately proceeded in keeping you at at least three arms' lengths. I guess it should have been ten arms' lengths for you to have seen what was plainly in view, to have gotten the glaring message that I had no desire for anything to progress beyond what was appropriate. But does my minor overstep in correct conduct undermine every last other time when I truly tried to communicate what I could not state out loud? I would have loved to have said how I felt, to have expressed that I desired for you to stay away. But to my great disadvantage, I decided to maintain my silence while quietly wishing that you would come to your senses. I kept silent for fear of the repercussion and possibly being told that I was overreacting and that you were merely being friendly, though that was far from reality. At the end of the day, were you not the adult in the situation? Why would I, a teenage girl, have needed to say or explain that the way you behaved was far from sensible, let alone moral; that it was unwelcome and intolerable? Or did you so cling to that single incident I mentioned that it led you to think that your senseless actions were welcomed, despite the ninety-nine other times I attempted to get the message across that I wanted absolutely nothing to do with you? Does one time override the ninety-nine where I tried to clarify that I wanted nothing to do with you? Does it justify your deplorable decisions to defy what was right, disregard that you claimed to be in youth ministry and forget your marriage vows to your wife? Now that we're on the subject, I've often wondered what her problem was. She obviously saw your misconduct, yet never thought to stop you or at the very least intervene for me: a teenage girl who was on the receiving end of her disgusting husband's frequent advances. She's almost as unbelievable as you. She stood idly as you leered at me, lavished me with inappropriate and unwanted compliments, and never said anything to put you in check, even for the sake of her own self-respect. I guess she didn't mind you running around like a clown, grasping at what you shouldn't have and out on the prowl. This more than confounds me for numerous reasons. To begin with, didn't it vex her that your affections weren't only towards her, and to make matters worse, they were towards an underaged girl? Didn't it sicken her that her husband was a hypocrite to such a great extent that he held the position of a youth pastor, yet was actually after an underaged girl while he himself was in his mid thirties? Didn't she mind that the supposed man she was married to, the father of her daughter, exhibited predatory behavior? Was this never a cause for concern to her? I know she noticed all that occurred but for whatever reason decided to turn a blind eye to my plight that was at the hand of her sorry excuse of a man. Maybe she was used to this from seeing it times before: perhaps I wasn't the first one you had acted like this towards, which may very well be the case, because with predators it's seldom just one; the cycle goes on until enough is enough. But she should have still spoken up, if not for herself in regards to the disrespect she was being dealt, for the shy quiet girl her husband was brazenly after. Or is it that she was unaware of the extent of your dreadful intentions? You must be irked by being referred to as a predator several times, but if you look back and examine your actions, what else can you be seen as than such? You can claim that you were just being nice when you tried to offer me rides and said you could teach me how to drive, but thankfully I was not so naive to believe you. I could see that you had more in store for me if I had agreed to be alone with you like you clearly dreamed. Do you think I've forgotten the time you feigned interest in my height and said let's stand back to back, then intentionally came too close and brushed up against my behind? I'm not one for violence, but when I reflect on this, I want to break a lamp over your head, especially because you never owned up to your actions but actually tried and succeeded in making me feel guilty. You had some nerve. Instead of acknowledging that you were a perv for pursuing an underaged girl, you turned around and pointed a finger at me. The absurdity is beyond perplexing: it's vexing because you went on as though you had done nothing wrong; meanwhile I was left feeling ashamed and that I was to blame because of that single incident I mentioned, which I whole-heartedly regretted. Obviously because I was wrong in my conduct and also because it was the reason I felt that I should just keep quiet, that I had no right to say anything, that I should set the whole matter aside and put it behind. I honestly tried, but many a time something elicited these unpleasant memories; eventually my disgust and anger began to rise as I gradually realized that the fault was not mine, that all the while I had been eyed by a predator who knew very well what he was doing. You said it yourself that before you turned your life around and gave your life to Christ, your only goal when befriending a woman was to end up in bed with her. Maybe some of those old interests still lingered. Which helps to shed light on the reason why you actually tried to suggest that the Most High may have placed me into your life for your own twisted delight, because in your distorted mind, you might have still held the belief that females—even if they're underaged—exist only for your gratification, for the satiation of the sick appetite you still had inside and were unable to hide. When you made such a blatantly nonsensical suggestion, did it ever occur to you that maybe it was your own temptation that was getting the best of you and not that you were being given the okay to do what you knew you ought not to? It's stranger still because you talked about temptation yet didn't see this situation as an opportunity to exercise some self-control, evaluate your behavior and realize you were crossing lines that brought your character into question. Which brings up a question I've had: Did you see me as an easy target because you didn't see my father around, so you never worried about the possible repercussions of your foul behavior being found out? Or did you assume I had daddy issues and secretly hoped I would appreciate attention from a male twice my age? I wouldn't be surprised, because you seemed to have some funny ideas, another one of them being that ladies you deemed as attractive must be vapid and nothing more than an aesthetically pleasing exterior. I remember you tried to insinuate that I was materialistic, which is not at all the case and was simply based on my liking to dress nicely. By the way, I dress for myself and not for the sake of gaining attention from men or because I think that physical appearances matter more than anything else. I shouldn't even have to explain myself, but I thought I better set the record straight since you have a way of seeing things that's rather strange. I mean, you saw me as a conquest to bag, regardless of your marital status and the fact I was underaged and nearly twenty years younger than you. I can hardly conceive that I was so deceived to the point of believing that all the fault fell on me, though I was only a teen when you preyed on me, while you were in your mid thirties, married, and in youth ministry. But it can be difficult to see things clearly when you're in the situation. It's through time having passed and taking a step back that at last I saw the situation for what it was. It's through great frustration and an overflow of emotion from all the shame and blame I unfairly carried that I've been able to get to this point and finally find my voice that for so long was lost in a whirlwind of confusion, guilt, shame and blame, and something close to self-hate, courtesy of your masquerade as a man of integrity while you persistently preyed on me and ultimately led me to believe that I was to blame. Through my youthful innocence, you managed to keep me silent and wrapped up in shame. But I've come to discover that you're the one who ought to be ashamed for your many and reprehensible mistakes and the fact that you never took accountability for your actions. You had countless chances to try to rectify your wrongs and not one excuse to try to validate all that went on. But instead you chose to slither down the low road, even though as a pastor you are held to a higher standard. I guess your bloated ego told you that the rules don't apply to you. I pray that you've changed, for the sake and safety of other young girls, so that no one else has to endure your advances and consequently be left with shame and questions and an unyielding feeling that they brought the harassment upon themselves, just as I've felt. Logically I now know that I did no such thing, yet still there's a part of me that sometimes wonders if I did. When I listen to that part, I can't help but tell myself that this happened because I somehow brought it about; that it didn't happen to someone else, it happened to me because I was overly friendly, which was taken as flirty, when instead I should have been even more avoidant than I already had been, and maybe I should have even been a little mean, if that's what it took to relay the message to you. Thankfully I know this to be untrue, for the voice of reason intercepts and reminds me that apart from that one single time I've already mentioned, when I acted as I shouldn't have, I did my best to keep you at several arms' lengths and I carried myself with respect. With that being said, I'd like you to know that you no longer have me fooled. You were entirely to blame for your outrageous behavior and have no place to try and say otherwise. Dear David, you're disgusting and contradictory in regards to what you are versus what you claim to be. You're cowardly, slimy, and comically hypocritical. You ought to take an honest look at yourself and make some much needed changes and leave your alternate reality where females—regardless of their age—exist for your enjoyment. It's been a long time coming, but I can finally say that at last I've expressed all that needed to be said. I've done myself justice that has been long awaited and found the courage to say what I had so long suppressed.

DEAREST DAVID

Dearest David, I thought I was done after letter number one, but I've come to discover I've only just begun. I'm honestly stunned that of all occupations, you made the decision to become a youth pastor. It's probably safe to say that you claim to be following the calling of God, which I cannot refute because I don't know what you feel you've been told to do. But my question is: What went wrong, and when? How did you go from being a man on a mission to shepherd young souls and keep them on the straight and narrow to being a creep who made indecent advances towards a girl in her teens repeatedly, then refused to take accountability for your obvious misconduct? How you had the audacity to give biblical teachings while leering at me openly is far beyond me, just disgusting, and truly shocking. Did your spirit never stir, causing you to stop and ponder what you were up to and feel ashamed, then be pressed to promptly change your ways? How you could face yourself as you behaved so disgracefully is bewildering. Were you so double-minded that you were able to silence your conscience and give in to your perverse desires while we were literally in church? What adds to my astonishment is the location of your transgressions. You didn't decide to step out of line at just any place; the space that you chose was the house of the Lord, then carried on like everything was normal. It would have been just as immoral somewhere else, but this illustrated the gall you possessed. You somehow thought you were doing no wrong. You actually harassed me after sitting through a sermon, singing church hymns, and speaking on God's word—absurd doesn't describe this. Is it that you took leave of your senses once the service ended, or did you never have them to begin with? I'm inclined to lean towards the latter, since it was not long after we met that you began to give me unwanted attention. Thankfully one of us had self-respect and a functioning moral compass, though one would have sooner expected it to be you, a youth pastor with a wife and daughter, rather than me, someone in her teens. It's sickening to think that you thought you were fit to give others moral advice when you yourself were misguided on the very basics, such as decency, integrity, honesty, and marital loyalty. I'd be thankful to know what emboldened you to behave so strangely towards me even in the midst of your wife's presence as she held your daughter in her arms. Your interests were undignified on their own, but what made it all the more inappropriate was that all this took place in a house of worship and that you never seemed to mind that your wife was by your side or at least within sight and caring for your child. If you felt comfortable enough to act in the shameful manner that you did in church, of all places, I don't want to imagine how far you could have taken things in another setting, unless everything is the same to you and nothing is sacred, not a house of worship or your marriage. I know no one's perfect, but the word instructs us to treat the Lord with deep reverence and carry out our salvation with fear and trembling and to try to not be the cause for someone to stumble in their walk with God, especially those who are younger. As a pastor you must be well acquainted with all this, which brings me to the question: Why did you decide to let it all go to the wayside? You most likely know that the Bible also says that if you walk in the Spirit, you will not gratify the desires of the flesh, which is exactly what you tried time after time, after you likely denied the quiet voice inside telling you to stop forfeiting common sense as well as scriptural knowledge for the lies you tried to tell yourself. I'm sure you're familiar with Galatians 5 verse 22-23, which lists the fruits of the Spirit, the last one being self-control—so where was yours? One would think that a pastor would be filled with the spirit of God, and consequently exhibit more self-control. But you didn't; instead you chose to cross the boundaries between what was decent and what was not. As a servant leader, shouldn't you act as an example of what it means to carry yourself with respect and dignity? As a pastor in youth ministry, shouldn't you especially flee from temptation so that when you tell others to, you're free of hypocrisy? As a husband, don't you regard your wife highly enough to want to remain faithful even when you feel it's tough? Because I entirely doubt you would've if I had reciprocated your interest and, like you, lacked basic judgment. Moreover, your indecent advances were in fact acts of unfaithfulness, so you can't say that at least at the end of the day you remained faithful. Because if things had gone your way, you wouldn't be able to make an attempt at that false claim. As a father, couldn't you have bothered to take a step from your warped lens for even a moment in order to ponder the effect that an inappropriate relationship between a girl in her teens and someone in his thirties could have on her, or that you would not want someone to put your daughter in such a situation once she reached my age? You put me in quite a predicament, yet as a pastor, shouldn't you be one of the last causes for someone to have more problems? Shouldn't you aid in alleviating troubles as opposed to multiplying someone's woes? Shouldn't you walk your talk so what you preach isn't merely empty speech? Shouldn't you seek to be a beacon of light in someone's life and never the reason they feel the need to hide in darkness because of the shame and guilt you've wrongly burdened them with? As a pastor who ministers to youth especially, isn't your duty to your students to guide them towards the right things, not to possibly lead them adrift? You missed the mark, to say the least, more times than can be buried. What exacerbates your grave mistakes is your refusal to make things right. Sadly you lacked the guts to own up to all you had done, and perhaps your pridefulness played a large part in blinding you from the truth, which is that you were at fault, not me and certainly not God. A rather aggravating aspect of this horrid situation is the lasting impact that it's had on me. You sexually harassed me, yet made me feel guilty: guilty for bringing it upon myself, though that wasn't the case, and greatly ashamed over a mess I didn't create. Then when I finally came to the realization of the facts of the matter, that I had been preyed on by a crafty predator, I eventually grew so overwhelmed by the feeling that I was a bad person who was filled with unforgiveness and animosity because I couldn't quickly get past the sins you had committed towards me. Once again I was left feeling guilty for something I had not brought upon myself. Although I had learned by then that I wasn't at fault for what happened, I still went back and forth between this knowledge and thinking that I had been in the wrong. Then on top of this, I grappled with how badly I felt about myself because I couldn't instantly forgive and forget what should never have been. You weighed me down with heavy burdens brought upon by your transgressions; you stressed me out and left me heavy laden with shame I was never meant to carry. If you had been a decent man and pastor, you wouldn't have behaved in a way so disastrous. I can't speak on behalf of others, in regards to the impact you may have had on their lives, but in mine you added no value. However, there is definitely something I learned from you first hand, and that is: just because the position one holds comes with the assumption that they are honorable doesn't mean that they should be trusted, no matter how convincing the front they put up is, especially if they're in a position of leadership. Their words and actions should be carefully weighed lest they potentially lead anyone astray or if they're unable to lead anyone astray, such as in this case, lest they leave anyone in a dreadful situation. I've learned from you firsthand that someone can pretend to have your best interest in mind, only for you to find that what they say versus what they live entirely misalign. I learned from you firsthand that talk is cheap, since in no way did you practice what you preached. You contradicted yourself left, right, and center, yet had the nerve to give biblical lectures. While all that occurred is still sickening and bewildering, I've come to terms with the insight that harboring anger isn't the answer. I've made the difficult decision to forgive you, and I've learned for myself that it's like what is said, "By forgiving I set a prisoner free, only to discover the prisoner was me." My heart is still heavy from the weight of these burdensome memories, but I'm grateful to be heading in a positive direction, towards inner peace in regards to all this, finally free of the shame you wrongly burdened me with. Dearest David, you're grossly hypocritical and unfit to hold a position in youth ministry and perhaps any position where there are underaged girls present. Because who's to say you won't try this again? You have no business teaching others about morality when you have obvious problems you should address urgently. You can say that you've changed, but that's the claim that you made when you told us about when you got saved. So who's to say that's actually the case and that you're not one temptation away from making even worse mistakes? You've made it evident that you don't always mean what you say, so as to whether you're the same or changed, there's no guarantee, and when it comes to young souls, it's better to be safe than sorry rather than to roll the dice and let anyone else be put directly into harm's way. Dearest David, the way you behaved is absolutely disgraceful and you ought to be greatly ashamed. If you haven't already, I hope you seek the help that you clearly need without any further delay. I hope that you stop with your charades, own up to what you've done, and finally be honest with yourself regarding all that's taken place. I hope you make necessary changes within yourself for the sake of those who are vulnerable and their safety. Lastly, I hope you know that although you were successful in keeping me silent for a while through the use of guilt and misplaced shame, that is no longer the case. I've since been familiarized with the truth and know that I'm not at all to blame. With that final word, I conclude.

THE UNFATHOMABLE

I don't even know where to begin, because there's no sense to be made out of any of this. All I can start out by saying is that I wish you and your kind experience all the suffering hell and earth have to offer. I cannot fathom how you can actually commit such hideous crimes against a child and face yourself day after day. I'd rather die or even take my own life than even entertain such nauseating thoughts, which is why I can't understand how you could extend your disgusting hand to bring an innocent child harm rather than decide that was your life's end. How you can look at a child and think anything more than "Aaw, how cute" is far beyond me; I can't begin to wrap my head around it. How can you be so sick? It's dizzying. It's as though every screw in your convoluted brain is loose, every wire is faulty and misfiring, normal neurological pathways are dark and winding, every marble is missing, and everything that could possibly go wrong in your mind is going on all at once. Simply put, what's wrong with you? How can your mind be so labyrinthine to lead you to act out things so vile? How aren't you taken by waves of nausea at the thought of carrying out such putrid crimes against a child? How can you even stomach the thought of violating a child, let alone having the mind-boggling audacity to follow through with the sickening thoughts contrived by your serpentine mind? It doesn't make sense. How can you be so bereft of the most basic level of decency? How can you be pullulating with the most loathsome form of lunacy? What is it in you that doesn't function correctly? Is it that you're devoid of a moral compass or just a disgusting fool? I can't imagine how you can find it within yourself to carry out odious acts upon a child? You filthy waste of space. How can you be so hideously foul and not want to take your life every moment you're awake? There's no excuse for what you've done, even if the same thing happened to you. Wouldn't that cause you to want to run in the opposite direction at a speed so great, rather than continue the perverse cycle of abuse? I've asked this before, but I must ask again, what on earth is wrong with you? Is it that you're possessed or just that disgustingly insane on your own? I cannot comprehend how someone could possibly find pleasure from putting their hands on a minor; the thought of it makes me want to vomit. There's nothing more repulsive, and any half-decent person would agree. So how could you be such a scumbag, and disgusting, and dumb enough to do the unspeakable to me when I was just a toddler and possibly younger? Is it that you thought that just because you weren't bringing me physical injuries that you weren't in any wrong, because the harm that you caused me was far more repugnant, and the wounds you inflicted, though invisible, were just as real. Not to make light of the plight of others, but I would rather have received bruises than the corrosive wounds you left me with. I remember at the tender ages of five and six being filled with such an anger that didn't make sense. It wasn't until recently I discovered that it was due to what occurred at an age even more delicate. It was as though a storm used to rage inside of me during that time because my mind struggled to cope with what should have never happened. You may think that just because you didn't leave me with physical lacerations that no harm was done—but you left me with deeper cuts that were harder to heal. Thankfully the anger passed, but that wasn't the last of the problems you caused me. Your disgusting deeds left me with a deep-seated hatred and disgust towards women, and I couldn't place the reason why; all I knew was that women made me sick and that they weren't to be trusted. I'm grateful that those twisted sentiments weren't internalized, causing me to have the same distorted views towards myself. But do you know how burdensome it is to have an underlying distrust and disgust towards half the population and not know why, ignorant to the fact that it was due to a nasty thing like you lacking the basic decency to keep off of me when I was just a child? Unfortunately it didn't stop there: you even caused me to have strange aversions to things as mundane as lace under-wear, and also to not know why that, as a result of disgust, I would have to turn away when I passed the aisle with linge-rie? Little did I know it was because I was forced to see what eyes as young as mine should have been shielded from. Still it doesn't stop there: I didn't know it at the time but you were the reason I used to have incessant nightmares as a child. I always feared something was coming to get me, unbeknownst to me that it was because of the revolting demon that used to abuse me. You may think you did no harm just because I was too young to remember what happened, but you left me with a hefty load of trauma to work through. I know for a fact that you threatened me with violence because of a dream I had when I was three. You were wielding a knife before your bare breasts and blood was dripping from it and your chest. The expression on your disgusting, foolish face was expectant, as if to see what my reaction would be. That horrid image has remained embedded in my memory since, reminding me that you really are the devil in human skin. I can't imagine being so sick and not having a fervent death wish. It's funny, though: I don't hope you're dead; that's too easy. Instead I hope you're alive and unwell, "alive" and suffering—but of course far away from children. I hope you're plagued with guilt and unrest every time to try to lay down your wicked head. I hope you spend every waking moment riddled with shame and the most profound self-loathing. I hope your squalid mind spins ceaselessly, leaving you wondering if you'll ever know a moment's peace, and I hope you know what a truly putrid piece of garbage you are. No, I don't hope you're six feet under; I hope you're still around but being undone by the most hideous anxiety, reminding you of the crimes you committed against an innocent child. I hope the grisly anxiety you face is ten times as bad as that that I've had to brave, once again ignorant to the fact that it traces back to what should have never taken place. I hope that every one of your days are doleful, and that you always wake up more morose than the day before, and that your existence is nothing short of unbearable for the many tears you caused me as a child and for the tears I've shed even now after all these years. I hope you grow to be anguished by the pain of your abysmal mistakes and that you live in immense regret, day after dreadful day. I hope you're crushed under the weight of shame that never ceases to grow more insane in its weight. Even though I've mostly gotten over the aversions that I've had, as well as some of the traumas from the past, I still don't wish for you to know a moment's peace. Because there could never be an excuse for what you did or an explanation as to why you're so sick. Every time you cross my mind, I'm disgusted and taken aback. I will never be able to fathom how one can be so consumed by perversion to the point where they lack the basic decency that ordinary people have. What on earth could cause you to desire to seek to rob a child of their innocence is far beyond me; I'll never comprehend it, nor do I wish to. All I want to know is that you're having to endure an existence wrought with suffering, since it's nothing short of what you deserve. You disgusting, loathsome thing, don't think that you've gotten away with this; what goes around always comes around, that much I know to be true. So if you haven't already, just know, one day you are going to thoroughly reap what you've sown.

THE BREAKUP

With a heavy heart, I must accept it's now time to move on. I didn't foresee this part, but it's now clear: what we once had is gone. I thought we would always be together, but it seems that isn't so. I thought our friendship would last forever, but it feels as though we've reached the end of the road. You know, it actually feels like a breakup, not just the loss of a friend. It has all the sadness and emotional shake-up; I can hardly believe that what we had is at its end. I've done what I can to make this last, but it seems you're determined to leave us in the past. Although it pains me so to let you go, I know it's what I must do. I guess what holds me is the memories of the past, the laughs that we had, and our promises to always have each other's back, but it's time I stop prolonging the inevitable—I know we've reached the end of the road. We've reached the last leg of us being friends, but I'll have you know that I wish you well. I cherish the great times we shared and having had someone so trustworthy to confide in. I treasure how truly you cared and how there was no competition: we were always happy for each other's wins. I'll try to let go of this lingering sadness, when I think of how what we have is now growing stagnant. Instead I'll hold on to the years of happy tears from excessive laughter and encouragement that always came at the right moment. I'll try not to lament the loss of a friend but instead be glad for all that we had. I'll think of you fondly and send you love and be grateful for this friendship that was sent from above. Even though I'm now letting go, I want you to know that if you should ever find yourself in need of someone to lean on, you can reach out to me. I'll be there, just as in the past. I'll always care.

COLLIDED PATHS

It's hard to imagine that our brief interaction has had such a lasting impact on me, but that's the fact of the matter. What's more incredible is that the circumstances in which we met weren't favorable, yet I replay the memory of that day in my mind again and again, just to see you, and hear you, and hold on to a small bit of you. Strange as it may be, I must admit: I miss you. It even sounds funny to me, but something keeps me holding on, though I don't even know your name. I find it insane, but with increasing frequency, thoughts of you run through my brain incessantly. I fall asleep with you on my mind and think of you first thing when I rise. I wonder how you spend your days and what you like to do in your free time. I wonder what your likes and dislikes are and if some of mine and yours are similar. I want to know about your passions and favorite distractions, if you have any. I want to put a name to the handsome face whose image has grown a bit vague in my mind, and simply know the heart and soul who have somehow called out to me in a way I couldn't have foreseen. I want to know what's behind this fascination that I can't shake and in no way wish to. In short: I just want to know you.

SURPRISED AND INTRIGUED

It's not like me to fall like this. What I know about you is next to nothing, yet I can't get you off my mind. I think of you all the time and wonder what you're up to and just want to know more of what you're like. I know we've hardly interacted, but I have to ask, Do I ever cross your mind, even though it's been a while? Do you ever have imaginary conversations with me? When your mind wanders, does it tend to gravitate towards thoughts of me? Because that's been my reality with increasing frequency. I see you repeatedly throughout my day, in every way. Something always makes sure that you stay on my mind without fail. I'm not even sure what I'm hoping for, really; perhaps just that I'll happen to run into you and we'll engage in a conversation that'll cure my curiosity at the very least and possibly lead to something more. Because my heart has grown a bit anxious to know you and what the future may have in store.

JUST US

Sure, I look forward to traveling the world with you, to exploring the earth and all of her natural wonders. But it's more so the simple things that I look forward to, such as waking up next to you for the rest of our lives and falling asleep to the gentle sound of your breath. It's not only the thoughts of the places we'll go and the sights we'll see that excite me but the time we'll spend together during quiet evenings, just you and me making sweet memories. It's not so much the idea of us taking a glamorous vacation across the ocean that thrills me but picturing us in an intimate setting just relishing each other's company. These are the things that delight me and incite the warmest sentiments when I sit in reverie imagining our future and how it will be. It's not so much the idea of us seeking thrills or doing something wild for the sake of creating a memorable time but rather the thought of being wrapped in each other's arms that excites my heart. I just want to be with you and grow closer to you and see your beautiful smile. I want to learn about the experiences that have shaped you into the man you are today. I just want to hear the sound of your voice and get well acquainted with the feeling of your warm, tender embrace. When I picture our future together, these are the things that delight me and elicit the warmest sentiments when I sit in reverie envisioning our lives and how sweet it will be.

GOOD RIDDANCE

I just wanted to start out by saying thanks for nothing. You wasted my time and took me on quite a wild and unpleasant ride; all you did was lie and make my life harder left and right. You pretended to be a friend, when really you were the devil in disguise. I still don't know what your problem is. Is it that your sense of humor is so sick and sardonic that it actually leads you to gain pleasure from making people's lives harder? Or is it that you truly have nothing better to do with your life than create headache after headache, time after time? Whatever the reason is, it doesn't make sense, and you really ought to get your head checked. Thankfully our friendship was ephemeral, but if only it hadn't been at all—because a few months of you proved to be a few months too many. One would think that by you being the older one of us two, you'd be the one to exhibit more maturity than you have, but unfortunately it's as though you're still living out the terrible twos—except when it comes to your calculated manipulation. I would have walked away from the start if you hadn't left me in the dark in regards to who and what you really are, but sadly it took for some time to pass before your facade began to crack. You masqueraded as exactly what you aren't, and to my detriment I fell for your act.

You played the angel, when really you were Satan and made yourself out to be a sorry soul who just needed understanding. You took me by surprise, because usually I can smell a rat from a mile away and spot a snake while they're still at bay. But with you that wasn't the case: I've never met someone so skilled in deception, I'm glad to say. If only you hadn't managed to keep that mask on for as long as you did; it would have saved me so much time and frustration. I curse the day we met, because it's left me with regret. I regret the energy I spent on you and my time that you wasted. I could have been doing something productive or at the very least getting some rest. But instead I was wasting my breath on arguments you attempted to goad me into, one time after the next. I count it as such a blessing that I've never encountered someone like you, because I'll never get how someone can revel in regularly causing dissent: with you, there was truly no rest. I can't stand anything about you, from the circuitous way you speak to your pride, which has no peak. Your love of drama disgusts me, as does your combative attitude. I still don't understand what's with you. Wouldn't you rather have normal, peaceful interactions rather than vie for fights? It just doesn't make sense, but I know logic isn't your strong suit. Another thing that irks me about you is how your moods swing with the direction of the wind and how it's always one thing or another that sets you off for seemingly no reason. Honestly, doesn't it exhaust you to be the way you are? Because it really seems so tiring to be such a piece of work. You must grow tired, so why don't you just stop? Whatever silly gains you think you make can't outweigh the cost. I could go on about all that sets my teeth on edge about you, but I'd rather not; the list would be too long. There is one more thing that I really found annoying, and that is: if I were to have behaved the same outrageous way that you did towards me, I know very well you'd never let me hear the end of it, yet when it came to you, I was supposed to just take it as ordinary. Once again you make no sense. I don't know why you choose to be the way you are, but I know there's no room in my life for you to have a part. To my regret I can't undo the day we met. Knowing you has been taxing and definitely something to lament. Thankfully this relationship is finally at its end; may we never cross paths again. Good riddance.

STEADILY UNRAVELING

I used to be filled with the joy of living; now it feels like I'm merely existing. Even breathing is strained; I frequently ask myself whether I should go or stay. I know taking my life shouldn't be an option, but every day is laden with pain. My days are devoid of the vibrant hues that used to color my life. Now every day is painted in varying shades of gray, and I desperately wish and wait for rays of sunlight to penetrate the dark and heavy clouds looming over me, attempting to consume the hope I hold on to that things will improve in the foreseeable future and that dawn will break and all will finally be okay—the hope that this dark and strife-filled night will finally come to an end and be illuminated by vibrant streams of light, beckoning me towards hoping again. It's not that I think it impossible for things to improve; it's the question as to when that will be that plagues me. Every day bears the weight of twenty, and I can hardly dream of how I'll go on like this for much longer. By and by, I'm struggling to see the point of why I should even bother, for the sake of living to see another day teeming with suffering just like the previous ones? I'm done. I've had enough of living in survival mode. I want to thrive in every area of my life and no longer wait indefinitely for the ever-elusive daybreak I so desperately dream of. I thought that this tedious season of waiting would be over by now, but I'm still feeling just as in-between as ever, as each day and night drags on painfully, eating away at what remains of my will to live. I hate to complain, but I'm afraid I've reached my limits. If things don't drastically change soon, I fear what I might do. I try to remind myself to keep the faith and that weeping may endure for a night but joy comes with the morning, but I've been mourning for longer than I can say. I try to remind myself to keep the faith, but I can't remember the last time I didn't face trials of many kinds, along with acute anxiety. I try to remind myself to keep the faith, but I can't remember the last day I didn't face absurd attacks at every turn that seemed like they would never end. I know that these trials won't last for life, but I'm really feeling the heat, and this fire's threatening to consume me. I know things will change, but this windstorm of pain is throwing me every which way. I know that these hardships must come to an end, but all sorts of calamities have been raining down on me and the pour has been heavy. I feel like I'm drowning and like the torrents of mayhem around me may sweep over my head, leaving me fighting to breathe. I wonder what's next: will the earth beneath my feet open up and swallow me whole? I don't know, but at this point I wouldn't be entirely surprised, considering what I've been fighting. Every day is a battle fought tooth and nail, and I'm not sure how much longer I can continue on this way. Everything requires a pep talk, and I'm growing less and less convicted whether it's even worth it or not to put so much fight in when I don't even feel like I'm fully living. I know my beating heart is enough proof that I do have it in me to push through; otherwise, I wouldn't be here. It's just that I've been telling myself to persevere to the point where it's started to grow old. My spirit is weary, and my heart feels so heavy. My mind is anguished, and I feel I've reached my end. I don't know what to say except I hope I don't do something that I'll thoroughly regret. I don't know what to do except pray, and I do every day without fail. Yet things still aren't okay, and there are still Goliath-sized obstacles in my way. I'm coming to pieces, when instead I thought that by now I'd be watching things fall into place. I hope to wake from this dreadful nightmare at any moment, but to my dismay, it's not been a dream; it's my day to day. I'm not sure what haunts me more: the thought of tomorrow or the fact that my life is a shadow of what it once was, both are tormentous. Despite what it may seem from an onlooker's perspective, I'm coming apart at the seams. If this ghastly chapter doesn't quickly come to an end, it may just be the death of me—yet I can't help but think what a tragedy that would be. So in order to prevent that from coming to pass, I'll just have to choose to look for the best in everything, count my blessings, search for the purpose within the pain, and remind myself that even though I don't know what tomorrow holds, I know Who holds my tomorrow, and that is sufficient, even if I don't have the answer to every question. I know I am held; therefore I know everything will work out well.

UNFORESEEN CIRCUMSTANCES

This season of my life can best be described as unforeseen, to say the least: the upheavals that have sought to rob me of my stability and peace, as well as the endless obstacles that have always seemed to crop up when I thought that, at last, this season was done. I don't know what to make of any of this. I've been hit with nearly everything life can bring, and it's all happened so suddenly, with no foreshadowing. I don't know what to think. I'm losing my mind and patience; if things don't improve soon, I'm going to lose it. All around me things are crumbling, such as my peace of mind and happiness, and my hope for tomorrow being better than yesterday. I just need drastic change to sweep through my life, because I don't know how much longer I can put in so much fight. It's like I'm at war with an invisible force seeking to undo me, and every time I conquer one obstacle, I'm met with several more. Everything's being put to test: my faith, my resilience, and my strength; I don't know how much I have left. But I know some of these days are making me wish I were dead. Every one of these days and nights are more strenuous than the last, and I don't know how many times in a day I tell myself that this, too, shall pass. Lately, each time I do, it lacks more and more enthusiasm than in the past, unsurprisingly, considering the trajectory of things. I'm just so tired of putting all my might into just surviving life. I miss thriving and the times when I was so happy to be alive. It wasn't even that long ago, yet it feels like it's hardly possible to live in that state again. I've grown so accustomed to hardships that I've all but forgotten the feeling of ease. Each time I believe that it's finally safe to breathe, I'm met with trials that are more tiresome than the last ones. I try to relax and just be grateful for the day, but it's like I'm always walking on thin ice just waiting to give way. If you would have told me just a short while ago that this is what life would be like not long from then, I wouldn't have believed you; I would've said it can't be so. Now every day is almost like a starless night, devoid of even a glimmer of light. Even though I don't see a sign of much change in sight, I'll just have to trust that I'll be all right and give what remains of this season all my fight.

AM I THE ONLY ONE?

Am I the only one who finds myself afraid to be happy at times? I hope so, because it's an unsavory situation to be in, and one that I've found myself in more times than is right. It's like when things are finally going my way after a long string of hardships, anxiety starts to set in as I wonder how long it'll be before things start to fall apart around me. I almost start to tense up and hold my breath when good things begin to enter my life again, because at least when I'm not riding high and I'm met with new trials, I think, well, this is just more of what I've been facing—unlike when I'm happy and actually have something to lose. It's almost like I'm tempted to search for stress because when my mind is partially occupied by anticipated anxieties, I can't lose the peace I didn't entirely have to begin with. I know it's not the healthiest way to reason, but I can't help but think that at least if I'm not up I don't have a long way to go if I'm brought low. It's just that it can be so hard to learn to relax into happiness after growing so used to it often being followed by one hardship after the next. It can be so difficult to let yourself embrace ease when you've not known a great deal of peace, because the question that reflexively comes to mind is at what point and time will this good thing leave my life? It's not my intention to embrace a negative mindset or welcome hardships as soon as I see a sign of them; it's just that I find I can't help but think this way at times, in order to sort of guard my heart from the disappointment and sting of a nice thing exiting my life without a warning. Sometimes I even find it difficult to believe that I should relax and let myself embrace happiness for fear of it being snatched away, even though I know that because of this, I'm not fully experiencing it when it is present. So you know what? In order to no longer remain in a state of a life lived in unhealthy precaution, I'm going to toss all worries to the wind and just live.

THANK YOU

Thank You. I walked through the valley of the shadow of death, and You led me through that perilous place. I trekked indefinitely through that darkness, and You delivered me when I thought at last I had reached my end. I had all but forgotten the feeling of freedom until You carried me out of Egypt. I had grown so unfamiliar with the feeling of fully living until You came and breathed new life in me. Because of You I know that it's true that although weeping may endure for a night, joy comes with the morning, because You've turned my weeping into rejoicing. You made a way in the wilderness for me and filled me up when I was running on pretty much empty. You blessed me with beauty for ashes when I had grown so accustomed to hardships. You called me out of the realm of the dead and brought me back into the land of the living. When the devil had me deceived that You were against me, You shone Your light into my life and told me You were for me. It was then that I experienced a newfound hope, which lifted me out of great depths of sorrow. You're the reason I am still alive and can testify to Your faithfulness. For it is by Your loving kindness that I have not been consumed; Your mercies are new every morning, Your compassions fail not, and I can say that great is Your faithfulness. I don't like to look back on it, but there were times I when I questioned Your kindness: when the trials in my life were multiplying and it honestly seemed like I wouldn't make it through the night, when I was close to collapsing under the weight of the burdens I was carrying, and when I was eventually ending my prayers with the resigned plea for You to please take my life if You wouldn't take away my suffering, for You to please not wake me up in the morning if I was only going to endure another day of crushing anguish, and worst of all, when I felt that I was on my own, that You had forsaken me, and that I would have to live my life without Your guiding light and without the consolation of knowing that You're by my side. Thankfully You came and changed the situation. You lifted the burgeoning weights off my shoulders and replaced them with a lightness I didn't know I could experience. You made it so that I triumphed over the trials in my life and that, once again, I was so grateful to be alive. You snatched me from the fires that were raging from every side and delivered me from the flames before they could set me ablaze. You kept me amidst the storm and ensured that the waters did not sweep over me and that the howling winds did not knock me down. You walked me through fires, and I came out unscathed; instead of being bathed by raging flames, I was bathed by Your all-encompassing grace. You saved me when nothing else could, and for this I must proclaim that You are good. When I was in the lion's den, You shut the mouth of every lion, You lifted me from that pit and set me high upon a rock, then my head was exalted above the enemies that surrounded me. You prepared a table for me in the presence of my enemies, and because of Your mercy, I never missed a meal. You parted the sea for me so that I could walk into freedom; You spoke to the storm and it became still. When I found myself on shifting grounds, You steadied the earth beneath my feet. When I didn't know which direction to go in, You went before me and made the crooked path straight. When I was growing faint, You gave me the strength to keep on pressing ahead. When I was crushed in spirit, You blessed me with renewal, and now my cup overflows. When I was clothed in a heavy robe of sorrow, You lifted that garment from my tired shoulders and clothed me with joy instead. You made it so that I went from merely surviving to absolutely thriving. When I was facing my darkest hour, You came and turned night into day; because of You I was finally able to say, "Morning has broken, mourning has broken." When my life was crumbling like sand, You restored and fortified it like only You can. During the lows I learned that You're all I truly have, but also that because I have You, I have all I could possibly need, which is freeing because I know in You I will never lack. For You are more than sufficient in every circumstance, and because You are able to do exceedingly and abundantly beyond all we can ask or imagine, so I will continue to stand confidently on Your promises. For in You, all things are possible, whether it's the removal of a mountain or unthinkable renewal. Come what may, I will not be afraid, for You say that I need not do anything. I need only to be still, for You fight for me. So I will continue to place all my trust in You, safe in the knowledge that You'll see me through just as You always have in the past, because even though I was hard-pressed on every side, You ensured that I was never crushed. Even though I've seen my share of trials, You've delivered me from every one. I walked through the valley of the shadow of death, but because of You, that wasn't the end. Because of You, I no longer lament, I no longer shed excessive amounts of tears, I no longer dread the day before it breaks; instead I smile with every sunrise, and the many trials of yesterday no longer follow me. Thank You.

ABOUT THE AUTHOR

Elizabeth Rehemma was born in Kenya and grew up in the United States. She currently resides in California. Elizabeth's hobbies include playing the piano.